Franie's Zany Adventures In Chemoland

Franie's Zany Adventures In Chemoland

Best wishes for good health. Fran Jud 2010

Fran Miller Jud

Eloquent Books

Strategic Book Publishing
An imprint of Strategic Book Group
P.O. Box 333
Durham CT 06422
www.StrategicBookGroup.com

ISBN: 978-1-60860-867-6

Printed in the United States of America

Book Design: Stacie Tingen

This is not a work of fiction. All characters in the book are real and have either gladly given their permission to be included, or begged me to include them. Names, places, and incidents are as accurate as the writer's chemo-influenced memory can recall them, and any attempt to re-create them was totally intentional.

Note to readers: The spelling "G-D" throughout this story represents the deity as written in the traditional Jewish manner.

Franie's Zany Adventures In Chemoland

Fran Miller Jud, RN

A humorous, supportive, informative memoir for anyone who has been touched by cancer, loves someone with cancer, been a caregiver, or lives in a world where they fear they might get cancer. Over 1,300,000 people were diagnosed with cancer just this year!

Dedication

This book is dedicated, with much love, to five people:

Dad, Commander William Miller, USCG Retired—you instilled in me a love of words and their meanings, and encouraged me to use them in writing, just like you did.

Mom, Elizabeth (Betty) Miller—you left me with your gift of gab, your lust for life, and the embodiment of your tremendous spirit.

Thank you both. I know that you are smiling down.

Robert, my husband of thirty-two years—thank you, not only for your year-long devotion and first class care during my chemotherapy, but also for your deep and heartfelt love, and your support and encouragement while I was writing this book.

Jeremy and Zack, my wonderful sons—you have been my loyal supporters and my technical assistants. I love you both so much, and thank you for all your help.

All of you are a part of me, and I dedicate this book to you.

.

Acknowledgements

First, I acknowledge my faith and give thanks to G-D, who must have a plan for me. My physicians—my lifesavers—you are held right up there on my life's list, and I acknowledge your gift. Without your combined efforts, who knows what might be?

Dr. Barbarevech, Dr. Ruggiero, Dr. DelSerra, and Dr. Heim, I thank you for helping me stick around. Dr. Ross, you became my chemo-mentor and friend. Thank you, and stay healthy.

Liz, what can I say? You will always have a special place in my heart. Your gentleness and respect for my status as a nurse, combined with your finely honed nursing skills, makes you extraordinary. Michele, my voice of calm and sanity in a world suddenly turned upside down—thank you for always having the answers.

I want to acknowledge all of my angels, and everyone in the medical field who participated in my care in any way. Thanks go out to all of my wonderful neighbors for their many acts of kindness during this entire time, "Oh, yeah, and thanks for making me laugh when I made references to that infernal retained camera and its possible location."

I want to thank everyone at AEG for having faith in me, and publishing my story. Cindi, thanks for your patience and prompt responses, even when I was a bit anxious…

Patti, my dearest friend, chauffer, and bathroom locater, thanks for always being there through symptoms and testing, surgery and recovery and the long year of chemo. Yo (my New York tour guide, friend, pants zipper-upper, tree-trimmer, etc) and Roy, the first readers of the finished manuscript, thanks, I have used many of your suggestions. Leni, your friendship and great listening skills, even when I babbled incessantly, meant so much, for that and more, a simple "thanks so much!" Louise and ET, your contributions and advice were invaluable. Nancy, your professional and diligent editing was exceptional, as well as your thoughts on the manuscript, many of your ideas are here. Thank you, so much for all your time.

Cindy, you know what I thank you for from the very beginning! Later, your technical assistance literally saved me, or at least the book, I wonder if it will ever end? KB, you have always been there for me, and your creativity and friendship are very special. June, you patiently heard just about all my words as they spewed out of me, raw and disjointed at times. You loved them anyway, thanks for patiently listening. Karen, my brave friend, you know what your friendship has meant to me. I have dedicated a chapter to you, and wish you good luck as a new RN. Donna, we are linked through the telephone at times, and by many years of friendship. Heal and stay safe.

Susan, just the sound of your voice during some of my worst chemo moments was so uplifting; you always made me feel strong. Thanks for being my friend and for all your efforts with my completed manuscript. Edie, you are a friend of my heart, or, in your words, "a true friend." We have shared our lives since we were seventeen. Even though we have been separated by many miles, we will always be connected.

Last, but never least, I thank my handsome and loving husband and caregiver. While reading is a bit too sedentary for you, you still actually managed to finish the entire manuscript and even made astute corrections. Sorry for all the "Wonder Chicken" dinners and sandwiches while I was finishing up. Thank you from the depths of my heart. My two wonderful sons, I am blessed to have you. Thank you for your support, concern, and pride, I love you both so much!

Table of Contents

Part One

What a Life!

What a Love!

What the Hell?

Prologue

This is my memoir—a first-hand story about my experience of discovering and battling cancer. It is different and unusual because it is written by a nurse who, in the course of many years of experience, has cared for cancer patients.

My diagnosis did not strike out of the blue, like a bolt of lightning, but instead, was wrung out of technology's every gimmick, as if findings were some sort of medical debris squeezed from a scientific dishrag. However, technology is not the only path to a diagnosis. While there are many life-saving guidelines for routine cancer screening (which should be followed), you must still listen to your body's subtle messages rather than relying on screening alone. Paying careful attention to even the quietest internal hints of something askew in your body can save your life!

Many people ignore these subtle messages or forego screenings if they are, like me, a "middle-of-the-roader;" someone who practices moderation in life. However, even if you eat a healthy diet most of the time, watch your weight, keep stress to a tolerable threshold, and exercise, cancer can still happen to you. Even a perfect athlete, like my personal hero, Lance Armstrong, was not exempt. A huge advantage to living a rather healthy lifestyle is not that you are guaranteed perpetual health. Rather, it is that illness may strike less frequently, and when it does, you will be in optimal condition to fight the battle—and it may be the battle of your life, should you suddenly find yourself a soldier in the war against cancer.

As a nurse I knew the importance of exercise, and in 2003, I finally got myself moving. I began by just walking fast, and then progressed to a slow jog interspersed by walking. Eventually, I worked up to jogging three miles

3

a few times a week—no easy task, as I really hated it. This accomplishment was actually my preparation for an upcoming out-west adventure that included hiking to the bottom of the Grand Canyon and back up in the same day. The descent and vertical return climb would total more than twelve miles. My husband, a marathon runner, was always supportive and kept me company on many of my training runs, as this was a trip we had planned together for several years. When the time finally arrived, I felt fit and ready to face this exciting challenge.

The night before this adventure was also our twenty-sixth wedding anniversary. Even though we had agreed that the trip itself would be a mutual gift, I had arranged an additional surprise. I had secretly made reservations and paid for two nights and a sumptuous dinner at El Tovar, a romantic, historic hotel delicately perched on the South Rim of the Grand Canyon. It was a far cry from our usual economy lodgings at a Motel 6.

That evening we watched sunset colors play across the canyon, illuminating some areas as if lit from within, and plunging others into a deep palette of purples, indigo, cobalt, and even violet and salmon. It was spectacular, and the very idea that at 6:30 a.m. the next morning we would descend into that dark chasm was equally thrilling.

I've included this next little tidbit just to give you an idea of the kind of man I married (lucky me).

Just as the celebratory dessert arrived at our orchid-bedecked candlelit table, he handed me a small gold box (this from a man who considers a Timex Iron-Man watch fine jewelry). With the dramatic backdrop of ebbing colors tinting the Grand Canyon, I opened the box and discovered a beautiful diamond anniversary ring. I was overwhelmed, awestruck, and absolutely speechless . . . probably for the first time in my life.

The climb down the next day was leisurely and enjoyable. The temperature that morning was in the 50s (Fahrenheit) but we were prepared for a possible 100 degrees at the arid bottom of the canyon. By 1:30 p.m. that afternoon we were relaxing, just chilling out on an outcrop of rock watching the rich, chocolate-colored Colorado River rush by. The canyon walls rose magnificently above us over a mile high!

It approached 110 degrees in the oasis at the bottom of the canyon, and a little heat overload left me with really red cheeks and I was definitely more than "glistening." Salty rivulets traced myriad paths from my hairline, through the fine patina of dust on my face, and moistened my chest. It was a relief to finally eat, rest, and re-hydrate for our climb out of the canyon. After I quickly dipped my head into the water trough provided for the mules, I was relatively cool and ready to continue.

Now I share all this with you because, as tough as that long uphill switchback climb along Bright Angel Trail was, I did just fine, really well in fact, so, I guessed that all my exercise and preparations had paid off. We hugged the rock wall and carefully maneuvered past mules, laden with people and supplies, as their bristly tails flicked our faces and backpacks as they passed us on their way down. My husband would often look up with angst distorting his handsome face, and say, "Gee, I wish we were at the top already." It was tough going but exhilarating. Just as I felt we were almost there, I would look up only to see, looming way above us, tiny black specks dotting that impossibly distant skyline—hints of the tourists watching those brave souls foolhardy enough to attempt the steep climb. Finally, we reached the South Rim, exhausted but elated, as the sunset once again triggered the canyon's beautiful light show.

Over the coming days we resumed our journey, frequently interspersed with many miles of hiking throughout Bryce Canyon, Zion National Park, Yellowstone, and Sedona. On one of our longest treks, in Zion National Park, we experienced a very scary situation. Our barely discernable trail in a canyon suddenly vanished at the base of a wall of sandstone. We had been guided to this point only by periodic cairns (small piles of rocks resembling a miniature pyramid) that marked the trails in order to guide the hikers, but they had disappeared along with the trail itself. Some very frightening moments ticked by, seeming like an eternity, as we frantically searched for the missing trail. We had been forewarned by the rangers to get out of the canyon if a storm threatened. Suddenly, an ear-splitting clap of thunder banged into the canyon, reverberating off the walls and straight into my heart!! The fear galvanized me, and I gingerly picked my way, with utmost caution, up that sandstone face. With the agility of a mountain goat and the exuberance of the Energizer Bunny, I reached the top, looking about madly at the surroundings. Miraculously, and with great relief, I shouted down to my anxious husband that I had spotted the cairn—our personal Holy Grail, nestled near a crevice in the ancient stone face. This little stack of stones delivered us to an escape route leading out of the canyon to safety.

After this harrowing experience, I felt I had met the toughest challenges of my life. . . . But, oh, was I wrong!!

Chapter 1

The Beginning—I Think

To provide better insight into my physical status, I will share with you our first real travel adventure.

Our hiking venture out-west was actually our second "anniversary trip." Two years previously, in 2001, we had embarked on an Alaskan cruise, our first real get-away. During the cruise we renewed our vows on the Love Boat with massive icebergs majestically gliding by. Whales spouted their plumes of white steam-like vapor as if it represented a champagne geyser—in honor of our special event.

This trip entailed much more than just sitting on the ship's deck with a video camera and sipping Kahlua-laced hot chocolate, although we did that as well. We went sea kayaking to a glacier, in high winds and white caps, while eagles soared overhead. We also rode on horseback along an ancient glacial trail. It followed a salmon-filled river, and we were able to see a black bear with its cubs fishing along the far shore. In Ketchikan, we clambered over a bridge and down a rocky slope so my husband could fish for the wild leaping salmon, while I photographed him in action. He did indeed catch one, and in the process we narrowly escaped missing the ship!

After our return from the Grand Canyon trip, I spent the next two years planning and organizing the next one. It was to be a really amazing combination of intense physical activities, as well as five days of total relaxation on the beach in Costa Rica. As before, I did some jogging to build up my endurance, but now I added weight-training as well. I wanted to be fully prepared for whatever we might encounter while in this Central American paradise.

This journey began in 2005 with an unbelievably intimate escape to La Paz, a small resort jutting over the rainforest, about one hour north of San Jose, Costa Rica. This fantastic setting also afforded us miles of hiking along steep, mossy paths through Mother Nature's cooling mist. Along the way we were able to view five cascading waterfalls while gem-like humming birds and brilliant butterflies flitted before our eyes. The next morning, we completed this expedition with a wild white-water rafting trip down the Serapiqui River, as it slashed its way through the rugged rainforest floor.

All was well in this exotic environment, as we headed north in our rented jeep, ready to embrace our next adventure. We traveled more than half a day on roads that were mere dirt paths set precariously along mountain edges, until we finally arrived at the quaint little town of La Fortuna. We awoke early the next morning revived and eager to begin a guided mountain bike trek out to Arenal, an active volcano. It would be more than a twelve mile round trip over areas of gradual elevation. We were fortunate that the peak, only seen a few days of the year, was not only visible but actually spewing thick eruptions of dense white smoke. Seeing this, our destination became even more enticing.

I rode like Lance Armstrong (my obvious hero and cancer survivor), out to the rumbling, smoking volcano. We paused only briefly to observe a group of Howler monkeys; a bit like gorillas, only smaller—cavorting in the trees above our sweaty brows. *Oh, it's a piece of cake,* I thought to myself, as I completed the first half of the ride. However, much of the return trip was slightly uphill, with the temperature in the mid-nineties: that heat, coupled with air that was moist and steamy from the tropical humidity could really bog down one's lungs (or so a part of my brain tried to convince me). What a toll it took! My energy was sapped, and my breathing became rapid and shallow. As a Registered Nurse, with experience in recognizing these symptoms, I attributed my condition to dehydration and that unrelenting heat. Unwilling to quit, I continued to pedal sluggishly alongside the rescue van, even though I realized that my burning calf muscles had little fuel left. At last, depleted and drained, I miraculously reached the end of the ride. I dragged my exhausted and trembling body into the air-conditioned van to recuperate. Oddly enough, during this entire ride my husband seemed unfazed. He would pedal rapidly ahead for short distances, and then return to beg me to get into the van. After the trip, he even rode further ahead just to photograph the Coatis. They are little raccoon-like animals that frolicked along the side of the road.

Later that day I recovered my drained energy completely by soaking in the Tabacon Hot Springs. The water there is thermodynamically heated by the nearby volcano, ahh, hot and soothing. Of course, drinking two Pina Coladas also helped round out my recuperative experience! Relaxed and soothed, I didn't give my recent episode of shortness of breath and fatigue another thought.

The next day we drove from sea level, around the volcano and its lake, and spiraled higher and higher through numerous tiny towns and remote villages. Our goal was to reach the biological cloud forest, located over 5,000 feet in altitude, at Monteverde. This tiny mountaintop village was so primitive that you had to put toilet paper into the trashcan, not the toilet. Even so, it was a naturalist's delight. The Howler monkeys serenaded their mates with their guttural calls in the trees just outside our door, and the exotic sounds of tropical birds were everywhere. So exquisite were the flora and fauna of this cloud forest that an intricate system was erected to afford visitors an up close and personal experience. It consisted of a zip-line that was suspended throughout the treetops. Climbing up to the zip-line, and hanging from it while sliding along from suspension point to suspension point, visitors would be treated to an intimate view of the cloud-forest's beauty and inhabitants.

Okay, now we are getting to some pretty amazing physical feats. Yes, that was to be our next leg of this remarkable journey!

On a day when the sky was a cerulean blue, with post-card perfect jungle foliage surrounding us, we excitedly awaited our turn to be harnessed-up to the zip-line. The dense emerald jungle and its creatures beckoned to us as we prepared for our ride.

In the event you have not had the opportunity to do this, let me further explain just what this experience would entail. Imagine, if you can, tiny metal steps hammered into tree trunks, leading up to platforms high in the treetops. The platforms have cables traversing the jungle and river below, connecting the treetop platforms to each other. The cables originated at the absolute highest tree in the surrounding jungle providing a continually sloping downward line leading to the next platform. In this way, you are able to glide through an unimaginable assortment of sights, color, and sounds, of vibrant beauty.

The zip-line experience would start with the donning of a helmet and leather gloves (Those would be BRAKES!!). A harness would then be strapped across your chest, from which a D-ring protruded—(a really strong one we hoped!) The ring was then attached to a pulley that then clicked onto the wire, which was suspended above each platform. Hanging as comfortably as one could be from the D-ring, you would then slide along the zip-line at quite a clip, and slow yourself down only by using your gloves as you approached the next platform. Thankfully, I have no fear of heights, as does my husband, Bob, so I had eagerly anticipated this airborne adventure through the clouds.

To use the zip-line, it was necessary to first hike uphill along cobbled paths that meandered through the dense vegetation leading up to the platforms. As I climbed higher, I suddenly realized that I was becoming quite short of breath. Higher and higher, my breathing coming faster and faster (remember, I am a nurse of many years), I began to feel as if I was literally gasping for air. When I mentioned this to my husband, he said he was feeling it, too. "Maybe it's just the altitude," he suggested. So, I dismissed my concerns and focused on the excitement ahead.

Once we ascended the first and highest platform, I felt my heart beating like a trapped hummingbird inside my chest. Surely this was just due to my excitement and anticipation, I thought. The guide quickly grasped my D-ring . . . CLICK, ZIP, WHOOSH! I catapulted off the platform into mid-air then briskly hurtled down the cable. Suspended from the taut wire in a semi-seated position, with my speed controlled by the pressure exerted on the cable by my gloved hand, I glided past birds with every color and form of plumage as their sharp cries heralded my approach. My husband, albeit less eager about this adventure, joined me at the platform. There we would be re-hooked to the next taut zip-line and launched again. So it went, platform to platform, until we completed our last glide. Thankfully, we climbed down to the solid comfort of terra firma, still in one piece.

I totally loved the experience, but once again felt that odd shortness of breath returning as we walked across the suspension bridges that stretched above cascading waterfalls and rivers. Fortunately, the next drive on our journey took us spiraling back down the lush tropical mountainside. We passed through small towns and sprawling coffee bean plantations, which finally led us to the Pan-American "highway"—quite the misnomer for a small, two-lane road. Finally, dust laden and parched, we arrived at Playa Tamarindo (a beach) where we dined and reclined in our luxurious beachfront haven. Even though we strolled for miles each day along the barely populated beach, we also lolled on beach lounges just steps away from the gently lapping ocean. This stay provided a much-needed reprieve for my silently struggling body.

Our last day at the beach found us tanned and fully sated on a tropical breakfast of rice, beans, fresh pineapple, and mangos. We loaded the car and headed south along the spectacular coastline. The relaxing and interesting drive took us past pristine sugary beaches, adorned by the foamy pearls of the crystal-clear turquoise water. We traveled through little Spanish towns that looked more like abandoned movie sets than actual villages. Along this route we even stopped to snap (no pun intended) pictures of humongous crocodiles lazily sunning themselves along the banks of the Rio Tortocolo. It was like being a part of a National Geographic special from a safe distance, both wonderful and exciting.

Our last destination was designed to include a medley of zoological rarities. Passing through famous surfing towns we crossed over a bridge constructed of nothing more than widely spaced rotting wooden planks, which afforded us disconcertingly clear visibility of the water below. Thankfully, the bridge held and no crocs were seen beneath us as we drove into the scenic harbor town of Quepos.

Our awesome villa was nestled high above Manuel Antonio, the town and a natural wildlife preserve. The villa had a private porch that literally blended into the surrounding jungle. The first morning, while sipping rich, aromatic Costa Rican coffee on our totally private porch (clothing comfortably optional), the solitude was suddenly broken by an invading tribe of squeaking, chirping, curious spider monkeys. Some of them had tiny babies clinging to their fur. They were adorable to behold, and it was hard to believe that animals living in the wild could actually be seen that close. That experience alone made traveling such a great distance totally worthwhile.

Later that morning, during our guided tour through the wildlife preserve, we were fortunate to glimpse a large variety of rare and unusual animals. These included two and three-toed sloths, an anteater, a Jesus Christ Lizard (so named because it stands on its hind legs and walks across water when frightened), and three species of monkeys gathered at the same place at the same time. This was a really unusual occurrence, we were told.

During this entire time I felt fine—at least I did until our long climb up some steeply cantilevered stone steps. They were carved deeply into the side of the mountain, and led to an open-air restaurant situated at the very top. During this climb, I became so winded that I had to actually sit down on the steps to catch my breath. When I finally recovered, we continued on to the restaurant. There we were again entertained by the brave little band of spider monkeys. They boldly cavorted over our tables in search of food, which we surreptitiously provided.

The end of the beginning, and the realization that something was really wrong, began on our last evening in this jungle paradise. We had decided to walk straight up the mountain road, about a mile, to have dinner in the Airplane Restaurant. The restaurant was built inside and on the wings of an enormous B-51 cargo plane. It was a long, hot, uphill climb. During this walk a tight fist of pain suddenly gripped my chest, sucking the oxygen out of my lungs, and totally incapacitating me. I was immediately short of breath, sweating and clutching my chest, as I slid gently to the ground by the side of the road. It was REALLY SCARY! Clinging to my husband's hand, I literally prayed, hoping just to make it home before I had the "Big One" (a heart attack) in a primitive part of a foreign country. At that moment I fervently wished that I could just click my ruby slippers together and be transported out of Oz to home.

Now, I really had a mission. I needed to discover what was wrong with my heart!

Chapter 2

Home Again, Home Again—Let the Search Begin

I am sure my personal spiritual advisor (G-D), played a major role in all of this. We safely touched down at my Pennsylvania hometown airport, and I experienced no further chest pains or shortness of breath. I thought I must be okay, at least for the time being. Even so, the events during the trip had convinced me, ever the nurse, that I must have a blockage in one or more of the vessels in my heart. This was a logical conclusion, given the symptoms I had experienced and the suddenness of their onset.

With a firm determination to quickly root out my problem, I did not make an appointment with my wonderful family doctor, who I later regarded as one of my lifesavers. Instead, I went directly to my cardiologist, armed with an extensive list of recommended cardiac related blood-work—all suggested by me, of course. In my single-minded earnestness, I skipped over a most basic and most revealing blood test, the complete blood count (CBC).

Amazingly, all test results were reported as normal. So, I now concluded, my symptoms must have been the result of simple over-exertion coupled with high altitude, tropical heat, and humidity. That was in March of 2005.

Shortly thereafter, I joined my long-time Baltimore buddies, Edie and Susan, who drove two and a half hours to meet me at the famous

Hershey Spa. There, we relaxed and laughed, and I rewarded my body with a luxuriant wrap of cocoa; the scent and sensations were intoxicating and rejuvenating. While there we baked in the sauna and basked in the fragrant steam room. I even jogged a couple of miles on a treadmill and felt just fine!

On the day of my return, my husband and I picked up a new black Lab puppy we quickly dubbed "Mookie." She was a very hyper, high-spirited female. We hoped this new addition to the family would give longevity to our older yellow Lab, Bailey, and fill the void to come in the event our youngest son Zack moved to Florida to attend grad school—which was becoming an increasingly likely possibility.

Every day that I was not scheduled to work (I worked part-time as a pediatric nurse in one of our city's major hospitals), I took Mookie for energetic and increasingly longer walks. In the beginning I was very winded, feeling almost as if I were going to pass out. Over time, however, that feeling not only lessened but it eventually disappeared. So, I was okay, I decided (NOT!).

Both spring and summer passed uneventfully. My only reminder of a lingering problem arose while walking in the mall, or from the mall to the parking lot with my friends. On these occasions the old shortness of breath would return. That's when I would query my friends, "Are you feeling winded?"

"No" they always replied, leading me to surmise that I must simply be out of shape. Perhaps, I reasoned, it was because I had not worked out or really jogged since our trip to Costa Rica. (Denial? Me?)

I must interject here that my ultimate goal is to be a patient advocate. So, whether you are male or female, if you find yourself huffing and puffing while doing routine chores, please consult your family doctor right away. If you dash up the stairs to answer the phone and discover you are still short of breath while chatting (hello, that was me!), do not ignore this. It may be a warning sign, and your only key to early detection.

Later that summer our son Zack was accepted into a Biology PhD program in Florida. Our family nest finally emptied when he and his fiancé decided to make the leap and relocate to Florida.

Being loving parents, we decided to be an integral part of their move by driving the moving van from our house to their new destination.

Bob and I really bonded as we transported our son and his belongings, as well as his fiancé's things, to their first apartment.

That summer was a record breaker, as far as temperatures went. Much to our dismay, we didn't discover that the rented van had no air-conditioning until we were slogging through Virginia's 100-plus degree weather! Have you ever sat for hours on a vinyl seat with no air-conditioning? I sure did! I rediscovered the feeling of soggy diapers at every rest stop, because my legs and butt were soaked and my damp shorts clung to me in a most unflattering manner. Ah, but that is parental love.

Physically I seemed fine, even while dragging heavy furniture around and steam-cleaning others. I did notice that my emotions were out of kilter and I was experiencing a sense of emptiness, but surely that was to be expected.

The final blast to the remnants of our scattered nest occurred when our oldest (and newly married) son, Jeremy, followed his dream of working as a pilot. A job offer resulted in his relocation from nearby New Jersey to far away Colorado. He and his wife of just one year moved halfway across the country, encountering a fluke blizzard on their moving day. Now, any visits to or from either of our children would necessitate an airline flight.

Every year in the late fall my husband and I took a lovely road trip to a small town in northern New York so he could run a ten-K race (six miles). He did this while I jogged the two-mile fun run/walk. For crazy personal reasons (I don't know, maybe because my husband runs marathons?), I always ran really hard and usually beat the young moms with their jogging strollers, as well as the fast walking silver-haired population. Indeed, for the last two consecutive years I had been the first two-miler to cross the finish line: a small victory that was private and silent, as no one was watching other than the moms of the little ten and twelve year olds who forced my weary legs to pump like hell just to beat them.

This year my husband chose to stand at the very back of the pack of hyper-charged runners to start the race with me—the "fun runners," you see, started behind the real runners. Ultimately, it was a good thing he did! The blank gun's crack released the runners and we joined in at the rear. Surprisingly, I could barely even walk fast along the beautiful autumnal paths that gradually elevated into uphill climbs. My husband refused to branch off and run with the other runners, instead he remained by my side—again, thank goodness! Almost immediately, I felt sick and devastated, as the same feelings I had experienced in Costa Rica overtook my body once again. This triggered a realization of the obvious: something was REALLY wrong with my heart! (What, you heard that refrain already?)

The holiday season suddenly hurtled in like a freight train with no brakes. Zack was coming home for Christmas and the New Year, so any thoughts of medical problems were banished to the deepest recesses of my mind and replaced by pleasant thoughts and the practicality of making preparations. Perhaps my frenetic pace, as I cooked, baked, and cleaned, caused an adrenaline rush that served to camouflage my symptoms? Regardless, I somehow managed to summon the energy I needed to prepare for the upcoming festivities.

New Year's Eve was always a special event in our neighborhood. The ladies decked themselves out in glitter and glam, and the guys came along to imbibe the drinks and sample all the goodies. I was looking good, if I do say so myself, but there was a nagging worry tucked away in my grey matter about the amount of blush it took to bring a little color to my cheeks. Around this same time I noticed that my usually distinct bikini tan lines were absent. I have an olive-toned complexion, and we had been at the beach under the tropical sun for two weeks in Costa Rica . . . Hmmmm . . . that was so odd.

At the party several people remarked that I seemed subdued and not my usual fun-loving self. Actually, I thought I played my role well, dancing and gabbing. After all, my husband and son were there, so who wouldn't be joyous and lively? (Perhaps someone who had erratic heartbeats?) My son left for the airport at 8:00 a.m., and where do you think I was by 9:00 a.m.? Oh, that's right, at the cardiologist's again. Where else would you go with an out-of-control ticker?

Even a non-medical person can visualize the battery of tests that this visit generated. The final test on the agenda was the application of a Holter Monitor. Some of you may be familiar with this device. It is a twenty-four-hour miniature EKG machine, complete with leads placed across the chest and attached to the small, portable computer-like recorder. It is worn slung over your shoulder, just like one more fashion accessory. Now I desperately wanted those crazy beats to reveal themselves . . . and they did!

Given my persistent shortness of breath and those strangely irregular heartbeats, a pulmonary (lung) function test was scheduled next. This would provide my answer at last, I was sure. By the way, for those who are wondering, I had smoked only one pack of cigarettes in my entire life, during nursing school, just to make a statement. So I am a non-smoker, as is my husband. Now I was on a mission to hunt down the answer to these medical symptoms that plagued me! Something was unquestionably WRONG! I needed to discover what it was!

Chapter 3

Doctor Sherlock Holmes on the Ward

On January 19, 2006 I woke up at my normal ungodly hour of 4:55 a.m. to get ready for my stint on the Pediatrics ward. As usual, it was a busy, whirlwind of a day filled with all sorts of catastrophes. During the morning shift change report, I casually mentioned to my coworkers that I was still short of breath and experiencing rapid heartbeats. To my utter astonishment they said, "You look like crap, and your coloring is paler than a corpse!" Maybe I did seem a bit pale lately, but this was a particularly harsh evaluation. Could I really have a problem? Did I have something like hepatitis? Or worse? (Ever the nurse, potential diagnoses fairly flew through my mind.)

It was divine intervention, I am positive, when a few minutes later I looked up to see my very own personal doctor walk right through the ward doors. To me, he seemed to be bathed in a heavenly light. Could I have possibly summoned him through mental telepathy, so great was my need? As he was rushing on his way to check a patient (we occasionally do accept adults, too), I snagged him by an arm and nearly dragged him into the nearby medicine room. Now, don't imagine the television show "Grey's Anatomy," with its steamy back room scenes, for my purpose was purely non-lecherous. After voicing my complaints, he made a quick perusal of my eyes, gums, and skin. Then he wrote me a prescription to get lab work done—and a lot of it! (This time, however, the tests were not of my choosing, but his, thank goodness!) He admonished me to have the lab work completed immediately, and it was hard to argue as the hospital laboratory was conveniently on site. So, I guess there are some perks to working in a hospital setting and being a nurse. I took my break right away, and had my blood drawn, within ten minutes.

This had to be the most dramatic and cataclysmic moment of the past year's events! Shortly after my blood was drawn I got "stat-paged" to the front desk for a phone call. (*Stat* is a Latin abbreviation, which we have all heard on TV shows, that is used in hospitals when there is an urgent situation or emergency.) Well, you don't have to be a nurse to know that ain't good . . . Grabbing the phone, I heard Doctor Ruggiero, in a voice that was oddly more subdued than usual, tell me to sit down.

Now, you're probably thinking that I received a diagnosis of cancer right then and there, but, oh no, nothing could be that simple for me.

He said, "Franie, now we know why you are so short of breath. You have severe anemia, and I want to admit you for a blood transfusion." Confusion, incredulity, and anxiety competed with sweaty palms and a rapid heartbeat to make my breathing even more labored as I pondered this new dilemma. A-hah! That was the problem! I had anemia (a low red blood cell count), which could be quickly and easily treated with a blood transfusion. I was relieved to discover that it was a diagnosis I could live with . . . or so I thought at that moment.

As a nurse, I knew that anemia indicates a low hemoglobin level, as well. (Hemoglobin is the oxygen-carrying protein found in red blood cells.) A trauma patient, with severe injuries and bleeding (think of an emergency room with blood spilling from the gurney to puddle on the floor), would need a transfusion if their hemoglobin level was at or below eight. My level was six, and the normal range for a female is twelve to sixteen. So, I realized that hard work and healthy living may have helped my body to compensate and function on half the oxygen-carrying protein that would normally be circulating in my system.

Doctor Ruggiero decided that I also needed a consultation with a hematologist (a blood doctor), since I had no obvious bleeding anywhere. This specialist would be able to determine the cause of such a severe anemia, and then formulate a treatment plan. So, fortunately, we agreed to hold off the impending transfusion until I had that appointment. Dr. Ruggiero hastily scheduled it for the next day . . . incredible.

Well, with the prospect of significant medical intervention looming ahead of me, I did what any sane woman in my shoes would do . . . I made a hair appointment! I always wore my hair streaked with highlights, and sported cute seasonal nails. Wanting to retain a sense of the normal me, I got my hair done just before the medical appointment that would catapult me into the realm of patient—a distinctly uncomfortable place for any medical caregiver, and, given my nature, most especially me!

My husband left work early and picked me up at Joe's, who is my hairdresser of extraordinary talents. (He comes back into our story later on.) Looking pale, but none-the-less well groomed, I approached the anxiety-inducing structure that housed the Hematology/Oncology Consultants of NEPA. Ironically, at that very moment, I said, "Wow! I am so glad we only need the hematology service." I never gave any other possibilities a thought. With an eerily prophetic reply my husband added, "Gee, I hope we won't ever need the other one."

To my great surprise, and relief, the hematologist, Dr. Heim, did not appear to be the Machiavellian ogre that I had expected. He was benevolent, kind, and grandfatherly, as opposed to the type of character that I had imagined to be a hematologist/oncologist. Smiling, however, did not appear to be a part of his initial repertoire—perhaps that was an occupational hazard?

After a brief but auspicious conversation, my hematologist informed us that my blood levels were so low that I needed an IV (intravenous) iron infusion. Whether this would provide an immediate and total correction of the problem, or simply be like putting a finger in a leak in a dike remained to be seen.

Could this have been a premonitory event, and a foretelling of things to come? Regardless, a follow up appointment was made for the infusion treatment, and we left the building to head home and talk.

On the scheduled date to receive the iron, my husband and I again approached the building, but this time with much greater trepidation on both our parts. Now, I'll not go into great detail here, but I did receive the IV iron over the course of four hours, which was infused directly into my veins. It was not a fun way to pass the time, but it was deemed necessary. The results were dramatic. With restored hemoglobin and iron levels, I felt far better than I had in a long time, and I was hopeful that my life would now return to normal. However, Dr. Heim felt certain that there had to be some kind of underlying problem for me to have experienced such a drastic reduction in my blood counts. He pursued the underling cause of my anemia with a vengeance.

The next test I needed was a simple one, just a test for occult blood (*occult* means hidden) in the stool. This can help determine if any bleeding is occurring in the stomach or intestines. To provide a test sample, you just dab a little bit of stool on a paper test strip enclosed in the matchbook-like pack. We've all done this test, right? If not, this, too, is a life saving tool and should be a part of your yearly exam—particularly for those over fifty years of age.

This whole process was vaguely reminiscent of waiting for the results of a pregnancy test strip, with all of its implications. Well, I (ever the nurse) was confident mine would be negative . . . and all but one of six were negative. However, one strip did yield a positive result. Simply put, there was some blood present in my stool. Even so, I was still secure in my naïve belief that it was probably a false positive, likely, just due to hemorrhoids.

Thankfully, my oh-so-thorough hematologist then ordered a CT scan, along with a colonoscopy, and an esophagogastroduodenoscopy (EGD) exam—(the first is a scoping using a camera to view the large intestines, the second is also a visual exam, but of the upper G.I. tract, from mouth to stomach). He ordered these tests in an attempt to find the answers that hopefully, would solve the elusive mystery of my anemia. I reluctantly submitted to each of these procedures while dragging my feet and whining like a recalcitrant child. Let me say, that these tests can be life saving and that they are a piece of cake compared to a missed diagnosis. The message: don't skip these tests they could save your life.

Every test came back negative, just as I knew they would, with only the CT scan results still pending. The colon (the large intestine) was clean and clear, and there was no sign of bleeding in the esophagus or the stomach. What was left to explore, the twenty-six feet of small intestine? (Well, even *they* were evaluated during the CT scan.)

On February 23 I was at work, "doing my pediatrics thing," as I liked to say, and I was in a relatively carefree mood. I was definitely feeling better now that my blood deficiencies had been corrected. Once again, however, I was summoned to the front desk *Stat* to take an ominous phone call from my doctor. My anxiety grew as I headed for the phone. *Was that my temporarily absent shortness of breath returning?* I wondered, as I struggled to remain calm. Dr. Ruggiero informed me that the CT scan indicated a problem in the distal portion of the small intestine—which is the portion closest to the large intestine, but not visible by colonoscopy. The exact diagnostic wording was, "a circumferential thickening of the bowel wall," further tests are needed "to rule out inflammatory bowel disease verses malignancy."

A clanging alarm sounded in my skull and echoed through my rib cage, jolting my heart! At that instant the rational, professional part of my brain fairly shouted to me, *You have cancer!* I was frightened, depressed, and confused. Nevertheless, I buried these feelings and kept on working, almost as if I were on autopilot. I was bogged down by an unspoken fear but I couldn't allow it to immobilize me. I became withdrawn, with random thoughts of cancer drifting through my mind. Then I remembered that Dr. Ruggiero had also told me to contact a surgeon. I seized upon this as a way to regain control and get answers. The necessity of making that call suddenly yanked me back to reality and motivated me, dissipating my fear and replacing it with a determination to get to the root of this problem.

Chapter 4

The Four A's: Alarm, Anxiety, Apprehension, and Anemia (Again!)

While a dark and foreboding fear draped its chilling hold over me, I shakily dialed a surgeon, who was also a family friend. After informing him of my distressing CT scan results he expressed no urgency or alarm, and tried to allay my anxiety by explaining that, "tumors in that area are extremely rare." This was comforting to hear, though it did not extinguish my growing worries.

Have I mentioned that I am a rare bird? A bizarre form of cancer, oh sure that would happen to me! My zest for life and optimistic cheerful personality, topped off by a youthful outlook, may be why I dance to a different drummer. These very traits later proved to be beneficial while coping with chemotherapy. The CT scan results must have caused my brain to cease delivering happy hormones, because I became increasingly anxious and feared being shuttled off to surgery, which would really make my life hurtle out of control.

Of course the surgeon wanted more tests . . . and lots of them . . . what a surprise!

In light of my predicament and the rigid testing schedule that was now required, my husband regretfully cancelled our long-awaited trip to Cancun, Mexico. We had planned this trip for over a year, but unlike our other adventure trips, this one was intended strictly to provide us both with some much-needed relaxation. However, given my recent medical revelations, the trip no longer seemed possible. My husband explained to me that he had recurring visions of me being rushed into emergency surgery in Mexico, while the only thing he could say in Spanish was, "Como se llama?" ("What is your name?"). Definitely not much help.

Disappointment felt like an anchor that was dragging me down. I had waited with bated breath to languorously welcome the kiss of the sun like my love's caress, warming my face and body, ever healing and potent. With a great deal of effort, I left this ruminating, gloomy prospective behind me, and replaced it with a driving need to find the damn cause of the anemia and get on with life. Perhaps ignorance was bliss?

Surprisingly, during this period of dark unknown I conducted my life with an even greater than usual gusto, like a manic maestro in high gear. Life remained filled with work, interspersed with shopping and movies, my reading group, Tai Chi, nails, hair, and even a spa pedicure.

All while a silent killer secretly inhabited my body.

The testing regimen now escalated to even greater heights, alternating between liquid diets and mint-flavored chalk. I even choked down turpentine-like syrup used to illuminate the intestines during an obscure exam called a Meckle's scan. It was implemented to search out a particular diverticulum, which is an inflamed pocket in the wall of the bowel. During the scan, my arms had to remain pinned at my side, with my body held perfectly still. The machine reminded me of some long creature and it felt like I was being swallowed into its metal mouth. All the while my mind raced along, drumming out, "Be this, be this, be this . . ." in the hope that this would be the test that cleared everything up. Next test was the G.I. series which consisted of multiple x-rays that were captured while I was swallowing yet another charming libation. The test's screen displayed the organs in a ghostly white glow, from the mouth, down the esophagus, into the stomach, and through to the end of the small intestine. The radiologist seemed to hesitate over my lower right side, "Is that it? Do you see something?" I pleaded. "Not really," the radiologist intoned. "It looks like a prolonged intestinal contraction," he finally concluded. "Oh, just great," I muttered to myself in total exasperation. Yet another negative test . . .

It seemed that there was only one option left: virtual endoscopy. YIKES! Now, I wondered, what in the world was that? It turned out to be a technological miracle! Just like in the '70s movie, Fantastic Voyage, the doctors wanted me to swallow a large plastic capsule. However, it would not be piloted by miniaturized scientists, but instead would be propelled by the force of gravity and peristalsis (the rhythmic, contractions of the intestines that move digested food). Encased in this capsule would be a space-aged, miniature camera and a strobe light. The light, which was programmed to fire at two-second intervals as the endoscopic capsule camera traveled backward through the convoluted innards, would illuminate what it has just passed. A cluster of adhesive EKG-like patches would be applied to the skin around the abdomen at various points, and tiny wires from them enter a device that saves the images. After eight hours the unit is returned to the doctors in order to view and interpret the images obtained.

It all seemed pretty sci-fi and intimidating, but there was nothing pretty about the whole deal! The capsule was designed to leave the body naturally after a day or two (following a cup of coffee and reading the paper, if you get my drift).

I was reluctant to swallow this alien thing. First, a lot of questions had to be answered, and I would have to endure yet another limited and dissatisfying liquid diet for two more days.

While I hemmed and hawed and deliberated with myself deciding whether or not to swallow the endoscopic camera, an alarming development expedited matters.

It is rarely good news when your doctor calls you unsolicited and in the evening. Yet in my case, this pattern seemed habit forming. Apparently my blood work, which was repeated every four weeks, had once again alarmed my hematologist. Specifically, my hemoglobin level had taken another nosedive. I was severely anemic again, and another IV infusion of iron was needed right away. (Yeah, okay, but I still needed answers—like the cause of this problem! Why, oh, why?)

Chapter 5

New York, New York—the Calm Before the Storm

After being held captive once again, ensnared by the angry rust-red IV line for yet another four hours, it finally sank in that I would have to swallow my fears—literally—and swallow that damn camera. I would have to stop thinking about the what ifs, (of course it would come out . . . paranoid me) and just submit to the procedure. Having already received two infusions of iron, I was certain that receiving a third infusion was not high on my want-to-do list. Even so, before popping the camera "down the hatch" I wanted to talk to my brother, Stu, "the doctor."

He and my niece just happened to be going to New York to visit colleges only two and a half hours away from me, by bus. So, I decided to hop on the big "grey dog" bound for New York City, planning to hook up with them for a short visit and a free consultation regarding the endoscopic camera. Fortified by my recent iron infusion and resultant blood count boost, I opted to walk the twenty or so blocks from the New York Port Authority bus station to their hotel in the warm spring air. Dragging my suitcase over the uneven pavement, its clattering wheels elicited the refrain, "New York, New York . . ."

I soaked up the hustle and bustle of Manhattan like a sponge. The beehive like buzz of the city was nourishment to my soul. I felt energized as we dashed across packed streets just to sample gourmet popcorn, or to check out the latest fashions. During the day, delicious scents from the chocolate shop drew us in like a powerful magnet, and at night we took in the razzle-dazzle of a Broadway show, "Rent."

My brother and I talked at length, and he reassured me personally, by referring me to all the docs he knew who had previously taken that virtual endoscopic capsule camera themselves. Finally, my decision was made. I would ingest that infernal camera. After that, I decided, I would treat myself to another New York trip. We would see a comedy then, in order to laugh (both at the whole thing, and, just maybe, at myself!).

At last it was all arranged. My friend, Yo (short for Yolana), a feisty redheaded transplant from New York, would be my guide and companion. We would sample tasty delights and laugh through another show—a comedy, this time, for sure. We planned to depart after I was finished with the whole dreaded camera ordeal.

So, after my rainbow diet of Jell-O and varied juices for two more days, I bravely ventured into Dr. Barbarevech's office (my gastrointestinal doctor), where I asked a final round of questions. The most pressing one was, "What if the camera does not come out?" I watched the face of this man whom I had trusted with my entire family's insides, as I listened to his answer. "Well, this is almost unheard of . . . it's really very rare indeed, in fact, almost all of us in the office have taken it" or so he said. (There's that rare thing again, offering me little comfort.) "If that vastly remote possibility should occur," he added, "the camera could just be plucked out by way of colonoscopy forceps, or removed laparoscopically." (Surgically! OY VEY!)

I had finally run out of questions and excuses. So, on April 19, 2006, I did it! Let me tell you, there was really nothing to it—far easier than hiking to the bottom of the Grand Canyon and back up in the same day. Indeed, it was actually a pretty cool procedure. I just swallowed the capsule, which I was not sure would go down so well, and the detector pads were placed around my abdomen, and I was free to go anywhere until the monitoring time was up. So, off I dashed with my friend, Patti (also a nurse), for some therapeutic shopping while the camera whizzed through my innards and time flew by. The little red eye on the computer winked every two seconds, with each photo taken. I was actually feeling content at the conclusion of this eight-hour test.

When the leads were finally unplugged from the adhesive patches, I felt sure that an answer to my problem was imminent.

The virtual endoscopic procedure appeared to have gone well, and as far as I knew the camera had naturally exited through a southern aperture right on schedule (some people may see the expelled capsule, others may not). So, as promised, on April 22, Yo and I spent a most wonderful day in New York, despite high winds and a soaking downpour. We revisited the gourmet popcorn and chocolate shops, as well as an elegant café, and we did get to see a very funny Broadway show.

All was well as we boarded the bus that evening, laden with edible and non-edible souvenirs. However, by the time the bus returned home and spilled out its shoppers, I began to experience a gnawing discomfort in my stomach. Before long that discomfort dramatically escalated, resulting in a frenzied night of alternating positions assumed to relieve the symptoms and interspersed with frequent trips to the porcelain throne. I was so sick! At first I thought it must be something I had gobbled down in New York, but when the illness persisted and I could not keep a thing down, I finally contacted my G.I. doctor, reassuring Dr. B.

He promptly ordered an abdominal x-ray and after receiving it, I was instructed to personally bring it right to him. Although I figured I could never decipher its results, I sneaked a peek anyway. Oh my G-D! There it was, looking like a bullet, that stupid camera—it was still inside me! Boy did that ever figure!

The results of the photo images from the camera exhibited inflammation of the small bowel. With these results, and my night of vomiting, pain, and now the retained camera, I was immediately admitted to the hospital into a room on my pediatric unit (at my request). At age fifty-nine I had only been a patient twice before in my life, both times just for childbirth, so I had always been blessed with good health, but apparently that was destined to change.

Upon further evaluation, it was determined that the camera had apparently caused an intestinal blockage, which was the source of my post–New York pain. After a few days of nothing but ice chips, I was feeling a good deal better. All treatment now, would be focused on the camera (no pun intended) and expediting its departure. Following those first days of ice chips I was finally issued the ultimate gift: permission to have a cup of coffee along with my mineral oil chaser. That should do it or else we could always try dynamite . . .

My caring hubby only left my bedside to feed Mookie and Bailey, or to bring me a cappuccino with whipped cream (nectar of the gods), but all to no avail. The camera remained firmly lodged inside.

Late at night my friendly IV pole companion and I would invade the nursing station, where I would glibly bend over and say to the girls, "Smile you're on Candid Camera!" Even after this hospital admission, those words remained a catch phrase often repeated as long as the camera continued to reside inside of me.

Daily radiographic studies indicated some movement of the capsule. My wonderful surgeon, Dr. DelSerra, finally allowed me to go home after a week of this involuntary incarceration. I left with a light heart and an armload of tongue depressors, and a little plastic toilet insert to assist me in camera retrieval.

It was business as usual the following week, except for the addition to my morning toilet routine—a kind of hunt and peck process that never resulted in retrieving the camera. While at work, I would slip down to the x-ray department in order to radiographically follow the progress of that lazy capsule. But, here's where the issue became complicated. (Like it has been simple up to now?) Various doctors and radiologists conferred about my x-ray results, and each developed a different opinion about the camera's movement. Some felt the camera was progressing slowly; others were convinced it was in the large intestine and would be outward bound at any time. My dear surgeon, however, was convinced that it had not moved at all. (Now who gave him a crystal ball?) The following weekend after my discharge, and a week before my sixtieth birthday, I was stricken again— this time really sick!

Since my husband had refused to make a big deal out of my personal big deal—I had arranged with all my neighbors (the New Year's Eve crew) to meet for dinner and celebrate my big six-o birthday. As that Friday approached, my increasing abdominal symptoms caused me, reluctantly, to cancel the dinner. This latest bout of misery resulted in a new test: a gastrograph. It was a really detailed x-ray, taken in combination with fluoroscopy. Once again, I just held my nose and slowly sucked down the necessary contrast liquid, while the mantra *the camera moved, the camera moved* rumbled around my head.

The next day I could finally eat solid food, and boy did I ever! I met my friend, Patti, at the local diner and I really pigged out. During our outing, however, my cell phone clamored for my attention, heralding bad news. My G.I. doc, good old Dr. B again, had read the results of the gastrograph and not only had the camera not budged, it was now apparently encased in fat—a bad thing . . . a very bad thing. They needed to schedule surgery immediately to remove the camera. "I just ate," I complained. "Well, then it must be scheduled for Thursday," he informed me. *Oh no! It can't be on Thursday, May 11, that's the day before my big birthday . . . this just can't happen . . . not on my sixtieth birthday!*

My husband promised we would do something really special the week after my birthday. (Obviously, following the upcoming surgery, if I would relent and schedule it.) I hemmed and hawed, pouted and prayed, and finally scheduled the surgery to remove the camera for 1:00 p.m. on Thursday, May 11, 2006. I thought about birthday cake and I wondered if I would be able to eat it the next day, but I didn't dwell on the impending surgery then. The surgery was necessary because the camera, now in my body three weeks, was trapped in my small intestines at a spot close to the large intestine but not retrievable by a colonoscopy.

How odd that the camera seemed wedged at the precise location the CT scan dubbed as "a problem" . . . where it indicated there appeared to be, a circumferential thickening of the bowel wall. At that minute, I briefly thought about the phrase "rule out inflammatory bowel disease versus malignancy," but then my mind raced over that, and traveled at lightning speed through endless and increasingly more anxiety-producing possible operative scenerios.

Chapter 6

The Final Kodak Moment

The morning of May 11 dawned beautifully and uncharacteristically warm, with the sky washed a pristine blue. The evening before, my husband and I had shared our "last supper" (for awhile, anyway). We ate voraciously, especially me, as I was not allowed to eat anything after midnight. Medically, this is referred to as N.P.O., (from the Latin, meaning nothing by mouth.) My surgery was not scheduled to begin until 1:00 p.m. the next afternoon, so I did not have to arrive at the hospital until noon.

With the morning to ourselves, my husband and I, along with Bailey and Mookie, headed to the field near our house for a bit of much needed pre-op recreation. The leaves, loaded with the chlorophyll charge of early spring, softly unfolded in the warm, nurturing sunshine. I tilted my face up to the sun and felt every pore absorbing its golden rays. Much like the early buds surrounding me, I felt my heart opening and an irrepressible zest for life filling it up. *This will be okay,* I silently reassured myself.

The dogs chased neophyte butterflies and insects, newly liberated from their pre- natal environments. It was such a joy to walk effortlessly for over an hour, without feeling shortness of breath or experiencing a cardiac rhythm gone awry.

It was as if I was suddenly gifted with super-human powers of observation. I could visualize the delicate shading in the throats of the spring flowers. Their sweet fragrances wafted to my nostrils and delighted my olfactory senses. My ears were serenaded by the myriad sounds arising from the trilling, chirping, squawking creatures living in the freshly dressed trees and bushes there.

All too soon, the time to leave the verdant field descended upon us. My husband and I then responded to a silent message that has telegraphed easily between us for over twenty-eight years. Turning to each other, we embraced tenderly and kissed deeply, even hungrily—each of us hoping for more—and not willing to relinquish our precious hold on permanence and security. Walking hand in hand, with my small, cold one enfolded in his big warm one, and accompanied by man's best friends (and woman's too), we strolled leisurely out of the field as if we didn't have a care in the world—a mutually adopted optimistic (albeit false) attitude.

Once home, I dawdled, savoring the comforts and scents of my home, until the last possible second demanded that we head to the hospital. My husband, lover, best friend, and soon to be caregiver and chauffeur, deposited my bright little lavender suitcase and a not-so-bright me into the car for this somewhat somber drive. I was a surgical virgin, naively hoping that my surgery would be simple, painless, and fast, and my stay very brief. (Am I really a nurse?)

While waiting in the anxiety-provoking waiting room, I became inpatient and took a little stroll. While on this brief jaunt, to my great relief, I encountered my surgeon, Dr. DelSerra, just as he was about to enter the operating area. We briefly discussed the proposed surgical procedure— "Removal of Retained Endoscopic Camera" and/or "Bowel Resection." I freaked out at this unexpected second possibility! He calmly stated that it was entered on the surgical consent form only as a contingency, just in case he "got in and the situation made it necessary to perform additional surgery." (A bowel-resection is the surgical term for removing any portion of the bowel or intestines.) I returned to the waiting room and again resumed my clock-watching. Finally, they called my name and my steady heart rate broke into a brisk trot. I reached for Bob and we hugged tightly and kissed again, open-mouthed and gentle—once, twice, three times— and then I was whisked away to Pre-Op. I had no idea that I would not see his handsome face again until late that night.

I am writing this in graphic detail, not to scare but to inform, and prepare you for any eventuality that you may encounter. If surgery is part of your treatment, discuss your pain relief options with your surgeon in advance. You can, you know, and you MUST! Adequate pain control is an important part of a timely recovery. Unfortunately, at the time, that idea had not entered my mind.

I was floating on a raft, adrift on a beautiful deep blue sea beneath an inverted bowl of the same hue, feeling comfortable and peaceful, without a care in the world. Suddenly, an enormous double-rowed pair of razor sharp teeth appeared at the edge of my vision, just to my right. Just as swiftly, the hideous demon of the sea rose up and clamped down on me, trapping my flesh! My entire right side was caught between those dangerous, salty sea scalpels. The creature sawed away at me, dissecting my flesh, crunching through bone, then taking a huge bite out of me! Tears welled up in my eyes as I kicked out at the beast, attempting to release its terrifying hold on me. The sides of my raft turned into metal bars, absorbing the wrath of my seizing legs. My vision, clouded by the salt-water, could barely recognize the scene around me. Slowly, very slowly, I emerged from my anesthesia-induced nightmare, only to realize that the pain was real and agonizing—I was in the recovery room. Out of my peripheral vision I caught a glimpse of what appeared to be an angel, hovering in the corner, gently waving at me. It was actually my friend, Patti, coming to help me while I was in the recovery room, but they told her I was much too agitated for her to come in. I wasn't agitated, I was in PAIN!

As soon as he closed my incision, Dr. DelSerra met with an anxious and pale Bob in the waiting room. He had some very dramatic news to impart. He informed my shaky spouse that circumstances had required him to perform a right hemicolectomy (the medical term for a partial bowel resection or removal involving the right side). All told, he had to remove a foot and a half of large intestine and three feet of small intestine, along with the associated lymph nodes. He professionally informed my husband that "the whole area was visibly inflamed and had the distinctive odor of Crohn's Disease," which gave us a preliminary diagnosis of "Inflammatory Bowel Disease." He never saw or specifically removed the camera, instead he removed the whole area encasing it and all of the inflamed bowel tissue surrounding it.

We later learned that this decision was a life-saving choice on his part.

Per my request (okay, I begged), they did not place an N/G tube or a Foley catheter (the first tube goes through the nose to your stomach, the other tube stays in your bladder).

What a shock this surgery turned out to be!

After the hellfire of the recovery room had passed, and I managed a brief, but cognizant discussion with the anesthesiologist, my heart-wrenching pleas for more medication—anything at all to relieve my pain, must have been answered. Thankfully, I remembered nothing of the painful move from the recovery room bed to the gurney, or the long ride under glaring florescent lights. Finally, bumping into the elevator, we rode up to the fourth floor and I was moved once again into my bed.

There, I was to become a temporary prisoner of the Marquis de Sade, whose sadomasochistic specter haunted all my un-medicated moments.

My husband gripped my hand the entire way to my room, willing me to be all right and to resume my characteristic magpie-like chatter. He longed to hear me say something, anything, as opposed to my deep silence. I am not certain when I first drifted up and out of my short-lived reprieve from pain, but I realized it was dark outside and that it must have been late. I discovered my hand was clasped in my husband's tenacious grip. Like Aurora in the fairy tale "Sleeping Beauty," my prince's gentle kiss coaxed me into awareness and, unfortunately, returned me to agony. The morphine pump (which can provide fabulous pain relief for many people) was just not working for me. Despite activating the pump, using the hand-held device to the lockout point, I just could not achieve freedom from pain. I have probably administered morphine to hundreds of patients over my thirty-plus years of nursing. Within a matter of minutes, the grimacing rictus of pain had left their faces and they drifted peacefully off to sleep. Lucky them!

Remember that I had refused placement of a Foley catheter? Well, I was yanked from a few moments of opiate-induced hallucination to a reality that proved far worse. The nurses informed me that I had not urinated in the ensuing eight hours since my surgery. They now had the dreaded job of catheterizing me (temporarily placing a not-so-soft rubber tube into the bladder to drain urine). I literally guided them to the right spot, after a few failed attempts, and even checked on the amount of urine they obtained. When they were finished with their torture program, I began my broken-record of requests for more pain medication or, failing that, at least a big hammer to knock me out! Their response was that I would need to urinate in the next eight hours, or this torture would have to be repeated. Urinate? I was just trying to breathe and exist. I obsessively squeezed the remote on the morphine pump, but to no avail.

Time passed, during which I drifted from crazed nightmares to an even crazier reality.

Clomp, clomp, clomp, the catheter Nazis marched into my dreams. It seemed only eight minutes, not eight hours, since they last violated me. How could these angels of mercy turn so cruelly into artisans of pain? I knew it was not their fault, but still . . . Could my dignity ever emerge intact from this intrusive prodding and probing of my most intimate parts? They left me with this final warning: if I did not "go" on my own in the next eight hours, I would have to have an indwelling Foley catheter inserted. (That is the tube that remains in the bladder.) NO WAY, JOSE!

Adrenalin surged through my drug-fogged brain, causing it to spring into action. I removed the morphine pump, and shoved it away, activating a chain reaction that was agonizing in its proportions. Now, maybe I could at least have some clarity with my pain. (Unless you are a medical person, and perhaps even then, don't remove a morphine pump; instead, get help.) The fracture pan, a plastic, wedge-shaped bedpan designed to slip easily under you, proved useless in my predicament. Thus, I requested a commode to be placed at my bedside (that's an adult potty chair). After several futile attempts, I finally managed to slowly drag my chopped carcass across the rough terrain of hospital sheeting and make contact with the commode seat. This maneuver finally resulted in a modest reward, a small golden trickle, but it was so satisfying.

Without the morphine haze, I realized that I had lost three whole days. My neighbor Terry, who was working in the hospital, had stopped in to see me, she later related, but I had no idea. Patti, my friend (and nurse with hidden wings and halo), administered to me the only cleansing ablutions I received during my entire hospitalization. Was the floor really so busy? Thank goodness for Patti, or I really would have been a dirty girl.

Her visit also provided Bob with a brief respite from his constant bedside vigil. Late that night, one of my co-workers, another real-life angel, Corrin, floated into the room and actually asked me about my pain level.

I told her it was unrelenting and she, smart girl that she was, noticed I had disconnected the morphine pump. Realizing that I was now entirely without any pharmaceutical assistance, she rushed into action. Propelled by my profound discomfort, she called my doctor and got a new medication order. That new medication, Dilaudid, entered my veins slowly as I silently prayed for a little relief. Ever so subtly, the hot knife in my lower abdomen seemed to melt, and I was left more relaxed and with only a hint of the intense pain I had been experiencing for days. She was a real angel, and a great nurse.

I share all this with you, not to fault the staff, but to urge you to become your own advocate and to request medication changes until you achieve true relief from the worst of your pain. If a Foley catheter is suggested, please accept it, as it is not as uncomfortable as having a painfully distended bladder after surgery. As you see, that can sometimes occur after surgery. A prepared patient can cope with surgery far more effectively, and recover much faster, than one who is not prepared. However, we can't prevent what we can't predict. So, a word to the wise, discuss your post-operative options and pain management plans with your doctor beforehand.

A strange coincidence developed during my stay. One month prior to my unexpected surgery, Dr. Ross, the head of pediatrics, was also hospitalized on our unit. He also had a cancerous tumor of the colon and subsequent hemicolectomy surgery. We all took turns administering to his needs. He, too, had a very tough post-operative period even though he was totally cooperative, unlike someone else. . . . Doctors and nurses are often non- compliant patients, as they may cope poorly with a personal loss of control in their own area of expertise . . . need I say more? At any rate, in the middle of my involuntary incarceration, on a day sufficiently blessed by Dilaudid which allowed me to put on clean PJs and hobble to a chair, Dr. Ross came to visit me. It was absurdly reassuring to see him after his surgery, dressed and ambulant, and looking great. Little did I know that he was soon to become my chemotherapy mentor, supporter, and a friend as well.

Many of my friends and family spent their valuable time at my bedside; a gesture that was deeply appreciated. There were many calls and visitors I was unaware of during those first three days. When I was told of them, it warmed my heart that so many people cared to check on me! My heartfelt thanks was (and is) extended to one and all!

One friend, who visited during that time, later shared this tale with me from those first, dark days. She was sitting by my bed, keeping vigil, one afternoon, when a nurse from the recovery room peeked in and requested a moment with the celebrity. I was apparently still quite out of it. My visitor queried her about her use of the word *celebrity*, and she was quick to explain my recent notoriety. Apparently my rare lodged-camera x-rays had been placed on a bulletin board in the recovery room. I had no idea that my personal Kodak moment had made me famous!

Other than the breaks provided when close friends visited, Bob was a permanent fixture in my room. One day, after I was finally permitted liquids, Bob joined me with his own meal that the hospital provided for him (a little perk of being a patient on pediatrics). At one point he plucked the lid from an orange sherbet cup. The sweet, citrus scent awakened my dormant taste buds. I blurted out, "Oh Bob, I need you, over here right now! You have to let me lick it, hurry! I want it so much!" The sudden smile that brightened his stressed out face, faded when I grabbed his hand and licked the sherbet lid clean . . . (Oh ye of dirty minds, not now, maybe never!)

Once I was again a "walkie-talkie," capable of ambulation and coherent speech, it dawned on me that my endoscopic camera was gone. It has been removed during surgery and I wanted it back, indeed I needed it back! After all, it had been a part of me for three weeks. In truth, it actually saved my life, although that fact was still unbeknownst to me. I relentlessly hounded the pathology lab, as Dr. DelSerra had confirmed that "patients have the right to obtain any material items removed from their body." (Do not even go there!) While still quite disabled physically, my mind raced along its own devious pathways, almost without my awareness. Multiple phone calls to the head of the laboratory initiated the proper procedure to grant my unusual request. I signed a ream of paperwork, goaded my shell-shocked hubby into a covert dash down to the basement labyrinth, which sequestered the pathology lab, and finally I regained possession of "my" camera—the one which I eventually attributed to saving my life. Now, however, it is always ON my person, not in it!

Chapter 7

Birthday Surprises . . . the Bad

Time indeed marches on, as it has a way of doing, and along with it, my dietary allotment moved up as well. As my dietary intake increased I felt a tad stronger, and by day four of my seven-day stay they actually managed to achieve a modicum of pain relief for me. One of my many angels brought me an IV injection of Dilaudid at 10:00 p.m., along with a Restoril capsule (a sleeping pill—which you'll need to ask for, too, if you're unable to fall asleep). By 11:00 p.m. I had fallen asleep, and I actually slept for at least five straight hours! Without the influence of morphine, my distorted impression of the world around me finally began to clear. At last I actually began to enjoy visits from my family and friends. Marie, the first person I met when I moved to Pennsylvania, and a very dear friend, visited and came bearing gifts. She brought me personality-perfect PJs—black and pink with flowers. Now I could maneuver around the ward in style and keep my butt covered at the same time.

The retained endoscopic camera became a standing joke and often some reference to it would be made upon first greeting me: "Ah, yes, you're the camera lady!" In light of that, late one night, I once again strutted down the hall to the nurse's station—as best as one can strut while pushing a co-dependent IV pole and supporting a slashed belly. Once there, seeing the brand new shift, I took my advantage, got everyone's attention, and bent over, aimed my bottom their way, and said, "Smile, you are on Candid Camera!" Yeah, I was still in lots of pain and had diarrhea, but I was living and laughing again, with a little memory of my old self flickering through it all.

At this point, I was diligently preparing myself to cope with the diagnosis of chronic inflammatory bowel disease and all that it would entail. I knew I could and would do just that, and, hopefully, slowly regain my pre-anemic, pre-surgical life.

May 17, 2006 was a big day! I was finally told I could eat a regular meal. I had been ordering a regular lunch or dinner for Bob, (thanks for that, Peds) along with my gelatin, soup, and juice entrées. Now I decided that we would have a celebratory dinner together, as the plan was to discharge me in the morning if I tolerated solid food. Solid food! HALLELUJAH! And, order I did. I was in "tapas" (several small samples) heaven, with a little of this, a little of that, and a whole lot of anything else I could find. Everything on their rather extensive (and good) menu was now at my disposal and I took full advantage of this opportunity. We closed my door and shared a wonderful, peaceful dinner; our banquet spread out on three bedside tables amidst a veritable florist shop of bouquets from friends and family. There was a whimsical floral arrangement from the girls on the floor in a giant coffee cup vase, trimmed with a big pink bow. (They knew I loved my java!) The room was filled with so many different species, from lovely plants to exotic orchids, that I really felt special.

Bob and I rested side by side in our matching geri-chairs, holding hands and feeling pleasantly sated after our hospital dinner of gourmet quality food (to me anyway). Recent surgery, coupled with the labor of eating so much, had exhausted me. So, with much less of my usual reluctance, I settled into bed with my ever-present caregiver by my side.

Suddenly, several loud raps on the door shattered our tranquility. I wondered, *What could possibly be in store for me now?* It was Dr. DelSerra, my surgeon, I expected that he had probably come by to discuss my discharge for the morning—at least this was what I then happily assumed. He strode into the room, garbed in his blue scrubs and, after greeting my husband, he perched on the window ledge about a foot away from me. He was neither cavalier nor inpatient, as he made comfortable small talk with both of us (a lovely and rare ability in a surgeon).

He first reassured me that my progress had been substantial—really good, in fact. At last he said, "We got back the pathology reports." His facial features remained neutral and revealed nothing, so we were prepared to receive my discharge orders. My husband softly implored, "So it's not the Big-C?" Dr. DelSerra then responded, matter-of-factly, "We had a problem. There was a cancer, and the camera had wedged against it. I got it all out, and the tissue margins around the cancer I had removed, were clear. I performed the surgery just as I would have if I had gone in knowing a tumor existed." He looked up toward the heavens and crossed himself as he said these words, a most endearing and heartfelt gesture.

All the air seemed to leave the room with his words. We were totally drained and depleted emotionally from his brief declaration. I JUST KNEW IT! I had felt it since January 19, 2006, from the CT scan results and now I automatically clicked into nurse mode.

"Will I need any further treatment, such as chemo or radiation?" I professionally questioned him.

"No, radiation will not be needed," he replied. "The tumor was extracted intact and I never opened the bowel, thank G-D. However, there were six lymph nodes, out of fifteen, that appeared to exhibit signs of cancer, so you will need chemotherapy." (Lymph nodes are often the first site to pick up any cancer cells that may break away or slough off from the main source of cancer.)

To this news I optimistically responded, "Well, the way I see things, there were nine non-involved lymph nodes, so that's good."

Dr. DelSerra was in total agreement with my positive perspective. In fact, he decided to discharge me that night instead of waiting until morning. He added that it might be depressing to remain in the hospital, and felt we would do better in our own home.

I secretly darted a quick glance at my beloved husband. He sat in utter shock, both mute and pale, as he desperately tried to contain his imminent tears. I tenderly stroked his cheek and told him that I would be fine. Then I turned to Dr. DelSerra and said, "If I can't get forty more years, I'll take thirty-five good ones." Pretty funny, I think, since he knew I'd just turned sixty the day after my surgery. That comment elicited a small chuckle and a response that he concurred. Bob robotically reviewed the discharge policy, post-operative instructions, and the list of medications. Oh yeah, baby, bring on the drugs! Keeping pain at bay was now very high on my priority list.

It was determined I would need another surgical procedure to insert a device through which I would receive my treatments (more on this later). The drugs used in bowel chemotherapy are very toxic to veins—in fact, to the whole body—this device would allow their administration while avoiding damage and reducing the discomfort of receiving the chemotherapy . . . In my case, chemotherapy would be administered over a course of twelve treatments. It was all okay by me. I just wanted to get out of the hospital at that point. Surprisingly, even though I was a nurse, I was simultaneously eager for discharge and yet apprehensive about being home with no medical backup.

Bob pulled the little red pediatrics wagon into the room and methodically loaded it up with flowers and plants, while I packed my suitcase for our departure. After numerous trips, he brought the car around to retrieve me—his wife, soul mate, and best friend. At that time I was still there for him . . . not totally the same person . . . but there, all the same.

What a shock it was to me that I needed to go out, not in a flame of glory, but in a freakin' wheelchair! Worse yet, use of the wheelchair was not solely a matter of hospital policy, but because I really needed one due to my own weakened and still pain-wracked state of affairs.

During the ride home, the knowledge that I had just had a cancerous tumor removed from deep within my body weighed as heavily upon us both. It was as if we had swallowed stones and they were lying in our bellies. Our hearts felt contracted, and Bob's tears slowly trickled out as if on their own volition, despite his futile efforts to stop them. Interestingly, I never shed a single tear!! Somehow I sensed in my core that I would be fine. G-D would not have stopped that incredible camera if he did not have a purpose for me. The adversities facing me would surely be overcome.

Paraphrasing the lyrics of a song, "I am woman, and I am strong!" Can you imagine? I had just turned sixty but I acted . . . hmmm . . . well a damn lot less— and though I only thought I was having minor surgery to remove a lodged camera, after which the first and worst surprise of my life had been dropped on me like a ton of bricks. No matter, this was NOT a doomsday prophesy—not to me! I felt sure of it. Dr. DelSerra had explained that I was in the best situation possible for a complete recovery. (I liked the way that man thinks.) Further, I was under seventy, had low blood pressure, no other medical problems (what, this is not enough?), and in great shape (or at least I *had* been in great shape).

The next step, he explained, would be to contact his office and schedule the insertion of a device through which I would receive chemotherapy. Once that was in, a two-week period would be required to allow for healing, and then the adventures in Chemoland would begin. Next I would have to make an appointment with Dr. Heim, my ex Hematologist, soon to be Oncologist. YIKES . . . there was that word! I simply refused to give fear a foothold in my brain. Yet, as another song lyric says, "What will be, will be," and I knew that I would be fine!

The appointment was made to get blood work drawn, and to discuss the strategies and the chemotherapy regime. Things were rushing along at top speed, but not me.

That first night at home, climbing (or perhaps inching would be more accurate) up the stairs, was really horrible. The pain, and my restlessness, were to be expected, just days after major bowel surgery. The next morning I made the painstaking trip down the stairs. I moved just as a toddler might—using one foot first, and slowly, following with the other. Once downstairs, I attempted to arrange a spot on the couch that was tolerable. Using several pillows, blankets, and a heating pad positioned over my incision, and with the help of my drugs (thank you, pharmaceuticals), I managed.

My husband, caregiver, and constant companion, set up a TV table and loaded it with snacks, real food, drinks, the remote control, and a slew of meds. Reluctantly, he finally returned to work, even though it was only for a half-day. There was no opportunity for fear, anxiety, or depression . . . just time to manage the pain, the pain, the pain.

Should you have surgery for cancer, let me share a pain-management strategy that might be a big help. Although you must always check with your doctor first, this can provide great relief. Make a warm compress by placing a damp washcloth in the microwave (for just thirty seconds or less). Then, put it into a baggie, cover it with a soft cloth, and gently place it over your incision . . . AHHH! What a difference this can make, such relief.

Chapter 8

Birthday Surprises—the Good and the Saintly

The next evening, May 18, 2006, marked my second day home from the hospital, and post-op day seven. My husband came home early from work (no surprise there) and prepared a light dinner for me. It was the most delicious grilled cheese I had ever tasted, far better than even a juicy Filet Mignon. I had just slipped into my couch cocoon, fully wrapped and feeling pretty good, with the drugs trying to do their thing, when I got my nightly call from our son, Zack. He asked me if I had been to the door yet, and noted that he had sent something to me by overnight mail.

Well that means it's probably outside the door right now, I was thinking to myself, as I began mentally counting how many steps retrieving it would require (Bob had just gone outside with the dogs). Next I found myself feeling upset that this struggling young couple had felt the need to spend any more money on me. They had already sent a beautiful floral arrangement, as had Jeremy and his wife. Surely they didn't need to do anything more. I was still lingering on the thought of the flowers when my son's somewhat demanding voice broke into my reverie. "Mom, you need to get it right away, it's perishable!" he implored.

Playing on his good spirit and sympathy, I whined, "Oh honey, your dad just took the dogs out and I am finally lying down, can I get it later?"

"NO!" he almost yelled, "Go get it now so it won't get ruined, and stay on the phone so I can hear if it is okay."

What choice did my battered body have? He was my baby, after all. I managed to schlep my diced, sliced, and drugged body off the couch, blathering away with him all the while. Then I hobbled to the door, still muttering that I wished he hadn't sent anything more. However, he seemed confident that I would like it. Slowly, ever so slowly, I found the reserve strength necessary for me to open the door. The entire time I was talking, I was also looking down for my mysterious package.

Gradually, a pair of boots came into focus, filled with . . . MY SON!

Okay, so I cried and sobbed and got completely out of control. Finally he said, "Okay, mom, you can hang up now!" His eyes were none too dry, either. We embraced—me, vigorously (forgetting for an instant the chop-shop hidden beneath my sweats), and he, very gingerly. That was a good . . . no, a great, wonderful birthday surprise! After that, it seemed that nothing could surprise me now . . . (HAH!)

During the night, slumber softly enveloped me, my pain ebbed away, and I slept the whole night through. "Endorphin release," would be the medical explanation, but I knew better. My son had come to see me, and he was back in the house. I was infused with an unheard-of level of post-operative energy, as I hobbled around the kitchen, weakly flipping pancakes. It was so great! I think my face ached more than my belly just from smiling so much.

Zack's fiancé came home with him and called me the next day. She wanted to say hello, and to convince me to take a short ride with her and her mom to check out a place for her bridal shower. Under normal circumstances, home from the hospital only four days, I wouldn't even consider a walk to the mailbox, much less a ride into town—even a very short one—but they had come home just to see me! "We won't be out long, will we?" I begged. "Only as long as you want," she responded. What could I do? Zack was going to meet us, and I was truly eager for more family bonding time, so it was soon all set.

As the time for our departure drew near, my son asked me, "Please do not wear those sweats. This is really a nice place, Mom."

Well, sweats had been my constant companions since surgery, and I wasn't sure about honoring this request. But, I figured, it couldn't really hurt to put on some regular clothes . . . could it? I soon had my answer: Oh yeah, it could! Pre-surgically, the time I required to prepare and leave the house was often as little as twenty minutes, from my shower to the front door. This, however, turned out to be quite a different ballgame. I was to be picked up at our house, so both Bob and Zack had gone out to do their thing . . . leaving me on my own.

My sanity was definitely in question as I painstakingly prepared for our brief outing. Thank goodness for elastic and drawstring waistbands—commodities I had previously never relied on. Bolstered by drugs (as prescribed by my surgeon), slightly enhanced by a bit of make-up, and held together with elastic, I was eventually dressed. I felt at least modestly presentable, and, equipped with my little pillow, I was ready to go.

Here's another tip that may be of great help, if you have to undergo surgery. Take a small camping-type pillow with you whenever you must move. Pressed firmly against your incision, it helps you to move with much less pain. It will likely be your constant companion over the next couple of weeks. During the ride, with my faithful pillow clutched against my belly, I thrilled to the beauty of spring emerging around me. It was really wonderful to be outdoors. Thanks to modern pharmacology, I was miraculously feeling fairly comfortable and actually looking forward to playing a role in the pre-nuptial planning. As soon as we pulled into the parking lot, I asked if anyone had an antacid, such as Tums. I didn't know if we would be sampling any food, but I didn't want to take a chance with my freshly sewn together insides.

Once we arrived at our destination, with pillow in place, I slowly crossed the parking lot to the door of the restaurant. . The hostess led us through an empty restaurant, down a dark hallway, and eventually to a door where I figured we would sit down and discuss the various options for the upcoming bridal shower. I had cautiously maneuvered my way to the dark door and pushed it open, when my senses were suddenly bombarded by a roaring avalanche of sound. "SURPRISE, SURPRISE!" The cheering assaulted my ears as lightning flashes from numerous cameras jolted my retinas. For a moment I stood motionless and uncomprehending, like a deer caught in the headlights of a car. Then my best friend, Edie, stepped up to me. I had thought she was in Baltimore, at a ball game with her grandchild. Next to her was my other dear friend from Baltimore, Susan.

Then Lyndyl and Barb, also from Baltimore and both of whom I have known for over forty years, filled my peripheral vision.

Family and friends were spilling out everywhere, and I was genuinely shocked, overwhelmed, and speechless—for only the second time in my life. Wisely, someone slipped a chair beneath my trembling legs, just in time. Multitudes of camera flashes ricocheted off dozens of gold and silver helium filled balloons, like so many floating bouquets. A fabulous fragrance floated in the air from a buffet table loaded with culinary delights, all sure to please even the most discerning palate. It smelled so good that I thought even I could eat something. Thankfully my son brought me a coke and admonished me to keep hydrated, as hoards of well wishers converged upon me.

It was not until much later that I saw the big poster. There I was in all my six-year-old glory, smiling my Mona Lisa smile, complete with bowl cut and bangs. All in attendance had written wonderful, celebratory messages around the edges. Reading their heartfelt get-well and birthday wishes, I felt my heart expanding.

Then there was the cake, complete with pink and lavender roses (my favorite colors). I was simply amazed that my husband had planned and organized this whole thing himself. Can you believe it? Long before any diagnosis or surgery, my dear husband, who stubbornly refused to acknowledge my big six-oh, had actually been planning a surprise party for me. On top of all that, he suddenly had to deal with surgery, my diagnosis of cancer, as well as deposits and deadlines. He seemed saintly to me now, as he attended to my needs, even personally bringing friends, neighbors, and relatives over to greet me. They came in ones and twos and threes, to wish me a happy sixtieth birthday.

Zack was there too, and he had announced to the anxious crowd, just moments before my arrival, "You can all kiss my mom, but please, no hugs!" He was ever diligent about my well being. Amazingly, I was able to eat a little of the delicate lemon-chicken and mashed potatoes, and even nibble on some other delectable dishes. Solid foods! Yet again, how delightful!

It was an outstanding, remarkable day, filled with smiles and tears. I was overjoyed and grateful just to be there and be surrounded by love. My son's sneaky visit was short, but oh, so sweet. What a warm and wonderful welcome home from the hospital this whole event turned out to be.

During the following week I returned to my chrysalis state. Curled around a heating pad and burrowed into the plush depths of the couch, I was slowly healing. Memories of the party flooded me with warmth. Only one thing was missing: I had so longed to see my son, Jeremy, and his wife. It seemed like they were the last piece to a puzzle, and that seeing them would give me a feeling of completion. They were coming east from Colorado to Maryland to take part in a wedding (which was why they could not fly back for my party the week before), but it was still more than four hours away from our home. I begged and cajoled, but the timing was just too tight.

Can you imagine my surprise (yeah, I know, again?) when the door opened as if by magic, and my wish came true? Jeremy and my daughter-in-law seemed to materialize before my very shocked and wet eyes . . . tears, tears, tears. How shamelessly they flowed these days, but tears of such great joy are good. They had managed to borrow a car and steal away in the wee hours of the morning, just to spend a few hours with me.

What wonderful medicine it was, and my heart felt so full. After another short but sweet visit, they left. No sooner had the door closed behind them than I felt bereft, missing them already. But now I could also bask in the warm afterglow of their time here. They left me with just one more teensy little reason to stick around—I was going to become a grandmother in early January, right about the time my first (and worst) round of chemo would be finished. WOW!

Preparing to fight the battle ahead was reminiscent of a soldier girding up for war. The kisses, the hugs, the love, and support flow over a young warrior, providing him with additional armor needed to help him fight with everything he has. With family and friends behind me, and the expectation of my first grandchild, I too, was ready to enter into battle, in my own personal war against cancer.

* * *

At this point in time, only my husband knew that I'd had a cancerous tumor removed and would need chemotherapy. No one at the party had any notion that there was more going on than the abdominal surgery I had just undergone. With careful and optimistic wording, I was able to share this information with my beloved sons. I needed time to process just what all this entailed before I was ready to divulge this most significant news to anyone else. Plans needed to be developed, actions set into motion.

I would first meet with Dr. Heim, who was now to be my Oncologist, and learn what his game plan would entail. (My very own cancer specialist . . . boy, is that ever eerie.) Next, I would need to schedule an appointment at Sloan-Kettering Memorial Hospital in New York City, one of the nations leading cancer research and treatment facilities. There, I would receive a second opinion and compare game plans. We were both really nervous about this appointment because I did have lymph node involvement and chemotherapy would have to be very aggressive and initiated quickly. I would also have to finalize the decision to have a device surgically implanted to facilitate intravenous (IV) chemotherapy. There are numerous methods available to help prevent damage to the veins, and make the administration of chemotherapeutic agents much easier and less uncomfortable. I planned to learn as much as could about these choices.

Chapter 9

New York, Again—What, No Show?

My appointment with a colon/intestine specialist at Sloan-Kettering in New York City was scheduled for June 7. I was only four weeks post-op, but I felt a compelling need to get the ball rolling. Like a yoga mantra, a message kept juggling around in my brain: *Get started on chemo, get started on chemo.* I felt an urgency to begin, a desperate need to regain some control in my life, and therefore, maybe get back to normal.

The morning we were to leave for New York was unseasonably grey, gloomy, and rainy. It seemed a perfect reflection of my thoughts. We were both oddly quiet and introspective during the drive into the city. The rain, falling in grey sheets at times, enveloped the car and muffled our thoughts, which were bouncing around in the silence. I was preoccupied, wondering what might actually be in store for me and my body. Bob's thoughts were a mirror image to mine, although he was also preoccupied with thoughts about how he could best help me to get through chemotherapy.

We intentionally talked of mundane things, carefully avoiding the purpose of the day's trip to New York, as it was definitely not to see a musical. This appointment would mold my future days, my next six months to a year—and possibly the rest of my life. The regimen for the best chemotherapy protocol available would be established at this juncture. My hopes were that the famous physicians of Sloan-Kettering Memorial Hospital would, somehow, be on the same page as my oncologist Dr. Heim. I desperately wanted to be close to home when I received my chemotherapy.

This would make it easier for me to deal with whatever unknown demons that might be unleashed upon me by the drugs. If the Sloan-Kettering physicians and Dr. Heim were in total agreement, I would almost certainly be able to receive my chemo treatments close to home.

After what seemed to be an interminable amount of time (though it was actually a record-breaking two hours), we spied, looming just ahead of us, the dreaded but necessary brown edifice housing the world famous cancer center. Unfamiliar with New York, we pulled into the first parking garage we encountered. There, we needed several minutes to recover from the sticker-shock of the cost-per-hour to simply park. Fortified by my prescription of "big white bombs" to hold back the surgical pain from my still-fresh incision, we headed uptown to our destination and my destiny.

The fierce wind seemed determined to undermine our progress, shoving us backwards with each step. Its strong fingers savagely inverted our umbrella, exposing its ribs, and us, to the cold, pelting rain. Bob, ever my he-man, gripped the umbrella and my arm and we boldly strode forward through the storm (both external and internal). For once, I could not match his stride, but barely hobbled along, clutching my ever-faithful pillow against my tender stomach. I was hunched over, looking like a little old hobbit scurrying for shelter and hoping for safety. The baby steps I managed did not exactly propel me forward, but eventually we entered the lobby of the awe-inspiring and anxiety-producing facility. Instinctively, Bob's grip on my hand tightened, sending its reassuring message, "I am here for you." My very first thought was, *Can everyone hear my heart beating?* Other thoughts followed in staccato blasts, so fast that I couldn't even sort them out. At last I took a deep, calming breath and focused on my mission: get seen, get chemotherapy, and get well.

Once inside the elevator, we were truly committed. I felt like Dorothy must have felt when she was heralded through the emerald gates to speak with the great Wizard of Oz. There was no yellow brick road to follow, but our path was made quite clear. I was astonished to see that every floor of the center was dedicated to cancer involving specific body parts. We bypassed the "breast floor" and the "lung floor," and then the "brain floor" (neuro). Finally, we disembarked on the "gastrointestinal/stomach" floor, also referred to as the G.I. floor.

Milling around us were beautiful, bald women, swathed under bold, brilliant scarves of every hue and texture. Others were wearing glorious hats, from pink baseball caps to sleek turban wraps. Other people roamed the halls making even more unusual fashion statements. I was later to learn that hidden beneath the leopard, feathered, bejeweled or leather accessories slung over their shoulders, were portable IV chemotherapy pumps. What a nice glamorous touch to chemotherapy.

After the expected ream of paperwork, and an unexpectedly short wait, we were ushered into an examination room (the inner sanctum of Oz?), to await the Great Wizard himself, or so it felt. First, I was interviewed by a double doctorate fellow (which means he is smart—really, really smart) who was doing research in the field of intestinal cancer. Man, that was comforting—right guy, right body part. He was so thorough that he recited my litany of shortness of breath, and the other symptoms that had occurred while zip-lining in Costa-Rica. It seemed he had reviewed and studied every facet of my symptomatology, in order to accumulate the most accurate information about my intestines (or what was left of them!).

Following this exam, I saw the prestigious Sloan-Kettering physician who only dealt with colon and intestinal cancers. Another reassuring and surprising fact was that my doctor was a woman. She examined me with sure gentle fingers, leaving no stone unturned and no bump or lump neglected. Her knowledge of the tiny details of my problems and surgery seemed extensive. She discussed my slides (more than thirty!) and told us I had a cancer called *adenocarcinoma.* She explained that it had been located in the small intestine, and subsequently removed.

We were then informed that this was a very rare form of cancer, due to its location.

Indeed, less than 1 percent of the population ever get cancer of the small bowel. (I told you I was a rare bird!) This apple-core adenocarcinoma was situated fifteen centimeters from the ileo-cecal valve (the valvular opening between the small bowel and the large intestine, or colon). That is the very spot where the camera was lodged. I just knew it! It was the same area that the CT scan had identified as a problem. The endoscopic camera was only able to photograph the large amount of inflammation produced in front of the lesion, as it was weighted and traveled backward capturing what it had just passed, until it stopped, wedged against the cancer . . . it's battery slowly fading.

The chemical cocktail she recommended included ten drugs—five primary chemotherapy drugs, and five supports. Thankfully, this was identical to Dr. Heim's recommendations. While not exactly exhilarated, I was truly buoyed up to learn that I could receive life-saving chemotherapy a mere five miles from my house, as opposed to traveling all the way into New York City for each infusion. Being able to receive chemotherapy close to home was major and just knowing that almost immediately began to lessen my anxiety.

The next step, she said, would be a PET scan. (First it was the CT or cat scan, and now it was the PET scan. (First, it's cats, now it's pets?) She further explained that this was a very advanced test that would identify locations of accelerated biological activity (cancer?), and pinpoint any tumors (cancer?). Then I would need a minor surgical procedure, during which, they would place a port, in order to gain direct access to a vein.

Because I have worked with them, I was familiar with many types of venous-access devices. My personal preference was a Port-A-Cath, which is surgically inserted under the skin and into the vena cava vein (a large vein leading to the heart). This particular device allows patients to continue most normal activities, including swimming, bathing, and exercising. They come in both single-lumen and double-lumen styles. That just means one has only one port for access, while the other has two, and consequently is larger.

As I am a small-boned, petite individual, to begin with, (and would probably get even smaller during chemo), my doctor there recommended the single-lumen for my situation. That same device is precisely what they use at Sloan-Kettering. Finally, she stated that the port should not be placed until after the PET scan, as this relatively new test is so sensitive that the presence of the port can alter the results.

At a point six to eight weeks after my surgery (the hemicolectomy), she recommended that I begin the intensive, chemotherapy protocol. The infusions would be given every other week for six months. Then, after a short break, she suggested an additional six months of one of the newer drugs in the group, Avastin, as an insurance policy of sorts.

By the time this extensive and very encouraging examination and consultation were completed, it was well into rush hour in the city. If we were to attempt to depart at this time, it would take more than an hour just to get from uptown, where we currently were, to the lower side of the city, heading home. Staff at the center suggested that instead we go across the street first and have some dinner, then we could relax a bit before starting our exodus. As if cued by a higher authority, the wind and rain abated just in time to allow us a more comfortable walk to a perfect restaurant, as we were rewarded by the beginnings of a sunset. The slowly deepening colors from the sun's last hurrah over the wet day, and its subtle hint of warmth as it sent the remaining grey clouds scuttling away, did much to warm our hearts on an otherwise rather bleak day.

The atmosphere at our table seemed oddly celebratory, I was on the mend, and surgically recovering well, and the pathology report indicated clear margins. This is a term often used regarding cancer surgery. It indicates that microscopic analysis of the outer edges (or margins) of the tissues removed showed no signs of cancer. Therefore, there was no spreading or *metastasis* of the cancer beyond the surgical area, and that the cancer has been entirely removed. I would still need the chemotherapy, because six out of fifteen lymph nodes were involved—though, to this day, I still say nine nodes were clear. That might just be an intrinsic aspect of my eternal optimism, but I believe it is a major weapon in the battle against cancer. Try to dwell on the positive factors in your life, as being optimistic has helped many people get through chemotherapy.

The soft flickering candlelight seemed to soothe away some of the stress of the day, and the quiet, padded décor cushioned our spirits, as well. We simultaneously reached across the table just to hold one another's hands, giving us immediate comfort. For the first time in quite a while I actually ate and enjoyed it! The big juicy hamburger stimulated my salivary glands, as I positively drooled at the sight of it. Though insufficient time had passed since my surgery for me to tolerate my favorite accompaniment to this meal (hot, crispy French Fries), the mashed potatoes substituted nicely. It was all washed down with a frosty root beer (as opposed to the other kind). Soon we were delightfully full and ready to tackle the long drive home. I felt fortified, and ready to travel the much longer road that still lay ahead of me.

If you or a loved one is diagnosed with cancer, no matter where you live, I suggest a trip to the closest major cancer center for a second opinion. This will afford you the opportunity to receive top-notch treatment and the best plan for success. In many cases, you can return to your hometown armed with the protocol from a famous center that your physician can follow, right in your own backyard, so to speak.

Once home, I would need the "PET thing" and the "port thing," so lots of research would be needed to provide me with information on the latest technology. There are many methods available to receive intravenous therapy. For some types of short-term chemotherapy, adequate IV access could require nothing more than having an intravenous catheter inserted into a vein. Placement of an IV is not too much different from having your blood drawn, and the catheter is immediately removed after the treatment is complete. In the case of long-term chemotherapy—I would receive twelve treatments, there are other alternatives available in order to enter a vein and avoid damage from the chemicals used . . . wonder drugs . . . you gotta wonder just what they will do to you! Your oncologist and or surgeon can make some suggestions and give full explanations, but you can make a decision based on what you feel is best suited to you. Sloan-Kettering recommended the single lumen Port-a-Cath (one site) device, and I also felt it to would be the best for me.

Once home, I was energized and ready to get going. I let Dr. Heim know that he was on the same exact wavelength as the cancer center in New York, and that he could now contact my insurance company to get required payment pre-authorization initiated.

This is an important detail. You must get your insurance coverage lined up, as chemotherapy is very expensive, but can you put a price on your life?

The PET scan was then scheduled for June 12, 2006, and two days later, during a minor surgical procedure, the requisite port would be inserted in preparation for the commencement of my chemotherapy.

Chapter 10

The Port of No Authority

After the trepidations surrounding my trip to Sloan-Kettering Memorial Hospital, I now had to cope with the PET scan, and the dreaded wait for the results. Then I could select and schedule the placement of the port. The PET scan, as medical procedures go, was relatively simple. The hardest part for me was the requirement to remain absolutely still, but I thought I could do it if I could just read a book. The test was geared to provide the maximum information about the biological activities unfolding inside the body.

So, with great haste, the test date was set and before I knew it, I was there. They efficiently started an IV (intravenous) in my arm. (No more IVs would be needed after placement of the port . . . hooray!) The IV drip delivered a fluid mixed with special sugars that would be absorbed first by those cells that exhibited accelerated biological activity. In other words, rapidly dividing cells absorb the sugar more quickly, while normally dividing cells are slower and more constant. The non-normal ones which demonstrate accelerated activity could be due to the presence of cancer.

All was going fine until I was instructed to remain perfectly still while the IV was infusing. The kicker? They took my book away! They said that even the minute movement of a finger turning a page was taboo, as "it could alter the test results." However, with great determination and tenacity, I made it! The test was completed and the results finally returned. It was negative, no cancer! YEAH!

They explained the results to me quite simply. Part of the test indicates the presence of actual tumors, and another part reveals the presence of any rapidly dividing microscopic cells of cancer, if they were present. Thankfully, for me, neither was found. I would still need chemotherapy as some lymph nodes had been involved, and chemo drugs are designed to seek and destroy even the tiniest of unwanted marauders.

The next step on my road to Chemoland would be the insertion of the port. There are numerous methods of direct access to the veins. If you are to receive a few, short-term treatments you may need only an IV catheter inserted by needle into the back of the hand, or into the arm to receive your chemo. An IV needle is used to make the actual puncture, but it is then withdrawn and only a very small, flexible plastic tube (IV catheter) is left in the vein. That, too, is then removed after the infusion is completed.

Another option may be a "central line," which is inserted into a neck vein via a needle which houses the thicker catheter tubing, allowing for safer and more comfortable administration of chemotherapy. The needle is then removed and a series of tubes with entry ports will remain out of the skin, but attached internally to the line. Usually a few sutures are used to hold a central line in place, leaving two or three catheter tubes each with injection ports, and their caps dangling.

While not usually recommended for very long-term treatments, this method of accessing a vein does work well for weeks, and does not require a surgical procedure to insert it. Lance Armstrong had his catheters (to receive his chemo), peeping out from his abdomen, which he referred to as his "pouch."

As a nurse, I was familiar with many forms of IV access and, indeed, had often used them to medicate my patients. However, from the prospective of chemotherapy patient, I had absolutely no experience. Thus, I did not have a clue about what it would feel like to have an in-dwelling device, or what would be the best kind for me. After reviewing as much information as possible, my decision was made, and a single lumen Port-a-Cath device seemed to be the best choice. This was the recommendation of Sloan-Kettering as well, and it would be completely self-contained beneath the skin.

Simply described, this device is a little larger than a nickel and about half an inch in depth with a tail-like catheter attached. There is also a double lumen version available, which looks a bit like two coins side-by-side, and is more than three inches wide. There is a border around the device, with openings that allow the surgeon to anchor the Port-a-Cath in place using internal sutures. The device is inserted (while you are under a light anesthesia) through an incision in the skin, usually beneath the collarbone and above the breast. The incision is just slightly larger than the Port-a-Cath itself, requiring about an inch for the single lumen device, and about four inches for the double lumen device. The tail-like catheter is then threaded under the skin and snaked into the Vena Cava vein. A small button-shaped mound is the only thing visible as a bump under the skin with the single lumen. Because it is entirely internalized, you can swim and bathe normally without any worry.

That was it, for me. I wanted a single lumen Port-a-Cath for my chemotherapy.

Next, I needed an appointment with Dr. Heim. Up until then, he had been my hematologist, but his new role would be that of oncologist . . . very scary indeed. My first oncology examination and meeting went well. Although it had been only five weeks since my surgery, I was already doing quite a bit for myself and my body was gradually mending. The great news, which Dr. Heim reiterated, was that the PET scan was negative for any evidence of tumors. However, I still needed the chemotherapy protocol of twelve treatments, because of the lymph node involvement. Each treatment would deliver ten drugs: five for chemotherapy, and five for support (either to help the chemo work, or to help me get through it).

Before my very first treatment could begin, I would need to have the Port-a-Cath surgically implanted. Initially, Dr. Heim informed me that they prefer the double lumen device. However, as a small-boned, petite woman, weighing 115 to 118 pounds, there was barely enough space on my little frame to place the single lumen device, much less the double! I also knew that weight loss is often inevitable during chemotherapy due to altered taste, possible nausea, vomiting, and even mouth sores, and this insight played a key role in my stubborn determination to receive only the single lumen port.

Dr. Heim and I discussed this at great length. He extolled the virtues of the double lumen port, emphasizing the immediate back-up access to your vein if one side becomes obstructed and cannot be used. If your doctor suggests a double lumen port, and you are not particularly small, then just go ahead and accept it, as it is a great device. However, if you happen to be small to begin with, you may want to voice your concern. I sure did! Remember, it's your body, and thus your choice! We did go around for a bit, but Dr. Heim finally yielded, as I remained unmovable. Even then, however, he stated that it "would only be okay with him, as long as my surgeon was in full agreement."

The Sloan-Kettering plan of action was to begin chemotherapy no later than eight weeks after the initial surgery. Well, I had no plans to wait around, twiddling my thumbs, while some microscopic errant cancer booger might be traveling around my insides searching for a home. I felt much like Lance Armstrong did during his fight: this cancer had picked the wrong body! After weathering my tortuous journey to Sloan-Kettering only four weeks after my surgery, I now felt much like a mailman: whether through wind, rain, sleet, or snow, the chemo must get through! I determinedly reiterated to myself. *Eight weeks, my ass!* I wanted to initiate chemotherapy by the fifth post-op week—the sooner the better! The faster the poison filled my veins, the faster it could begin its seek-and-destroy mission. Later, I would mentally picture a miniature army of toxins racing through my body with their high-tech weaponry, zapping anything that did not belong. Of course, some good things might have to go, too, but they would be welcomed back when the time was right.

It seemed my last obstacle was the actual surgical implantation of the port, and I was ready to hurdle that, full speed ahead!

June 12 was a delightfully mild day, in the mountains of Northeast Pennsylvania. There was just a hint of summer's hot breath stirring in the air as I arrived at my surgeon's office. This was my pre-surgical appointment for the Port-a-Cath placement. My initial surgery, completed on May 11, was barely four weeks behind me; I was attired in drawstring shorts and a tank top with a button styled shirt opened over top. That attire was not a fashion statement, but borne out of the desire to see exactly where the port would be placed, with the least amount of time wasted.

Here I'll offer you another suggestion: be sure you get to see in advance where the port or any other device will be placed on your body. You will need to be comfortable with it, as it may be your companion for a long time.

I also knew that I would be receiving chemotherapy all summer long, and I liked to wear tank tops when it was hot. So, I intentionally wore one that day to assist in the decision of location. I was mentally geared up to do battle, but I wasn't thinking for a minute I would actually encounter a problem.

Boy, was I wrong!

Dr. DelSerra was vehement that he always used a double lumen Port-a-Cath, and I was even more vehement that I would just have to break the mold, so to speak. Hoping to further his cause, he produced a sample of a double lumen port.

Holy cow! That sucker, to my anxious perspective, appeared magnified and much larger than it actually was. Trying very hard not to hyperventilate, I first whimpered, then kinda cried, and finally declared outright that I not only wanted but *needed* a single lumen device!

By means of reproach he said, "Well, if it becomes obstructed, it might require another surgery."

Even so, I could not be swayed from my decision. After quite a few rounds of discussion, Dr. DelSerra resignedly admitted that it was my body, after all, and my decision. (Please do not ever lose sight of that!) So, my single lumen Port-a-Cath device was finally scheduled to be surgically implanted on June 14, 2006.

Somehow, I was more eager than anxious when we once again found ourselves in the waiting area outside the operating room. At least this time I knew exactly what was going to be done, and the expected outcome. (You think?) This was the last remaining barrier to receiving my life-saving chemotherapy. Familiarity, in my case, breeds contentment, or at least a sense of control. I remembered what a difficult time the nurses had starting my pre-op intravenous line the last time I was there, so I told them, "You may not even try, please just get me the boss!" Whether I was a pain in the ass or a patient in control, you decide. I believe that we must all assert ourselves at times. The boss was fortuitously kind, understanding, and very skilled. Exhibiting considerable professional dexterity, the IV catheter seemed to just slip into my vein.

That simple act totally reassured me, and I felt positive that, this time, everything was going to go smoothly. Even though it was a relatively minor procedure, it was still surgery, and anything that helps to alleviate anxiety is good. I had not yet even received the little shot of joy juice that helps a patient to relax prior to surgery. It had to wait until I had talked with my surgeon and signed my permit.

When Dr. DelSerra came to my pre-op bedside, he had the requisite permit in hand. After reading it, however, I really flipped out! Get this! The operative permit stated, "Surgical insertion of DOUBLE LUMEN Port-a-Cath." So much for my calm confidence and serenity! Now I was definitely not calm—no, I was wild, actually. I less than serenely grabbed the proffered pen and demonically scratched through the word "DOUBLE," and wrote in big, dark letters the word, "SINGLE." Then, just in case, I underlined it a few times. (Can't you just see me now?) Before he could say a word, I etched my initials over the changes as is legally required (something I knew from years of experience).

Finally, in what I hoped was a strong, assertive voice (but which was, in reality, squeaky and on the verge of tears), I asked, "So that will be a single lumen, right?"

He shook his head as he replied, "I guess so."

Now that the formalities were over with, they began to wheel my gurney into the operating room. Striding by my side as we rolled down the operative corridor, Dr. DelSerra asked me if I was "ready to relinquish the reins."

"Umm, maybe one rein," I groggily replied, as they shot the sedative into me. With the resurgence of my humorous disposition, augmented by the drugs, I added with a soft chuckle, "Hey, you want to do a double? Okay, then make 'em really big and put one on each side!" Those were my last words as they pumped all the good stuff into me, inducing total oblivion.

We were home by two o'clock and I took up residence, once again, in my couch cocoon. My recovery after the port placement was surprisingly swift and nothing like the tortuous pain-filled events of the past.

The next day I was really sore, it sort of felt like a sharp jab to the chest, overlapped by a burning sensation, but it was manageable. I used my long-standing personal therapy to cope with this new onslaught to my body . . . I went shopping! Of course, I could not drive yet, so, once again, my angel, Patti, came through. She picked me up and off we went. The only time I actually complained about discomfort was when I moved clothes on the racks a little too vigorously. I did the best I could, knowing that my new port was there, silently mocking me, as it did not yet serve any purpose. I was eager to get on with it and get the chemo started. Yet, by the same token, I was also anxious and, if the truth be told, a little fearful of just what might happen to me and what I would have to deal with during my journey through Chemoland.

* * *

Life often runs in strange parallels. My very oldest friend (in terms of longevity of relationship, not age), Donna, called me from Baltimore. She sounded weird to me, bordering on hysteria. This was two days before my very first chemotherapy session was scheduled. Her voice was strained and clogged with unshed tears. Eventually, she managed to feed me bits and pieces of a horrible event she had barely lived through. Apparently, an intruder had broken into her home in the middle of the night and brutally assaulted her—much like the intruder that had broken into my body and assaulted me. She had just been discharged from the hospital, and was all alone. Her world was reeling, her body broken, and her spirit flagging.

I had been blessed and sustained through my events by my incredible husband, sons, and friends. Everyone needs someone at difficult times. Thus, I summoned my inner reserves of strength and natural compassion to comfort her. I was there to listen and commiserate with her despite, or perhaps because of, what I would be going through. As I suffered through the various stages of chemotherapy we would convene, each of us sharing with the other our diverse maladies, whether physical, mental, or emotional. Thus, a pattern was formed, as we each gave and received in spontaneous and reciprocal ways. I often remarked to her about the oddity of the timing of these events in our lives. Both of us were suffused with an unspoken need, which we somehow managed to answer for one another through the worst adversities, at times clinging to the phone like a life preserver.

* * *

By the following week, the site of my newly implanted port was still sore, but more tender then painful. It was now ready to serve as the portal to my body for the necessary chemotherapeutic agents, and I was ready to embark on my adventures in Chemoland. While there would be no maps or compasses to guide me, I was, nevertheless, well prepared as I had my soul mate by my side and faith in my heart. I was also blessed with children, family, and friends, who would be there for me if the road got too bumpy. Thankfully, I also had a zest for life and an abounding sense of optimism that began filling every nook and cranny of my being.

It was time to depart, the journey awaited. So, hand in hand, we were off to Chemoland.

Zip-lining in Costa Rica March 2005 The Beginning

Here I am with the camera somewhere inside me....

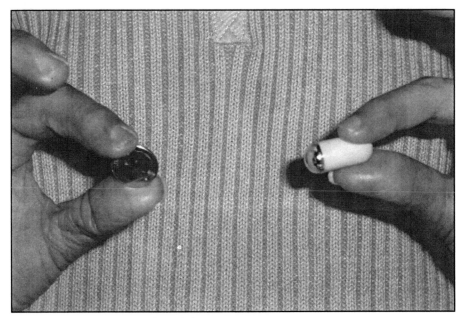

This is the camera--Retrieved much later!

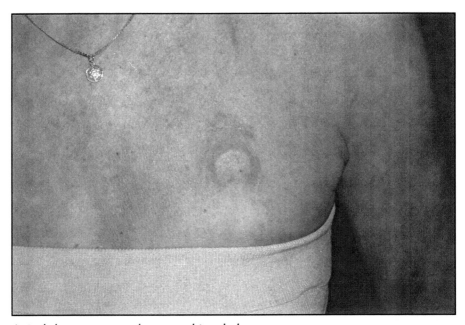

A single lumen port-a-cath, not too big a deal.

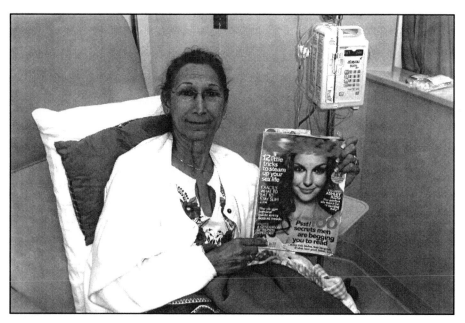

Franie during a typical chemo treatment.

September 7, 2007 Bob and Franie in Maui at Sunset; 1 year survivor-30 years married!

Part Two

Hand-in-Hand

Through Chemoland

A Little Heads Up, or a Brief Infomercial

Chemotherapy is a means to an end. A double-edged sword, it slashes away at deadly cancer cells while its rampant surge through the body, is unfortunately, indiscriminating, killing some healthy cells along the way. It robs you of your dignity, energy, hair, and normal lifestyle. Although you must tolerate the side effects that chemotherapy sows, you may then be entitled to reap the rewards of a lifetime. Literally, the reward may be your life! The side effects are numerous and varied, but there are many ways to assist you in gaining control over these frightening and unimaginable tortures. Being informed about them by your physician, or reading about them, (or, even BEING a nurse, or doctor) does not alleviate the anxiety of not knowing exactly what will occur to your body.

While each type of cancer may be treated with a different kind of chemotherapy, there is a common thread that runs through the lives of cancer patients, binding them together through similar experiences. Chemotherapy, regardless of the type of cancer and body part involved, causes some side effects, which seem to be universal in nature. For this reason, many recommendations and approaches to coping may also be universal.

For example, you should maintain a positive, optimistic outlook during chemotherapy. Doing so actually helps improve your immune system while releasing hormones in the brain, which may assist your body in dealing with some of the side effects. Along that line, try to develop a support system before starting your chemotherapy. Any person that cares about you, and who you can trust—be they a spouse, a significant other, brother, sister, neighbor, best friend, or a relative you can count on—will prove invaluable to you during your treatment. If you are able to find more than one person to assist you along this journey, even better, as the major caregiver will appreciate a break now and then.

Chemotherapy is a term used to describe a treatment of cancer with toxic drugs that attack cancer cells. All the cells in the body are produced, grow, and die according to a controlled pattern. Cancer causes certain cells to keep dividing and growing wildly multiplying out of control; these cells totally disregard the normal, ordered pattern of cell growth. Therefore, one of the main objectives of chemotherapy is to stop cancer cells from dividing and growing, thus destroying them.

Chemotherapy has been scientifically engineered to seek and destroy cells that are rapidly dividing. In this way, the greater toxic effects are borne by cancer cells rather than healthy cells. However, many of the body's healthy cells divide and multiply rapidly, as well, but according to a controlled and healthy pattern. Consequently, these healthy and normal, but also rapidly multiplying cells, have no special armor to provide protection, so they too are smitten by the chemo sword. The result of this deadly assault on healthy cells is referred to as chemo "side effects."

The destruction of healthy cells results in many problems and symptoms for the body. The type and dose of chemotherapy you receive, and how your body copes with it, will determine the specific side effects you will experience and their severity. Once chemotherapy is completed the normal cells slowly begin to recover, side effects gradually recede, and, over a period of time, healthy cells have the opportunity to resume their normal growth patterns. Many factors play into the amount of time it will take to get over the side effects. These include your overall health, age, length of chemo administration time, and the type of anti-cancer drugs you have been receiving.

The next portion of this story deals with my personal experiences during twelve rigorous chemotherapy sessions. Each person traveling through Chemoland will have an individualized itinerary and "trip ticket" to follow, guided by their doctor and their own body. While the going is bound to be tough, there are many ways to smooth this journey. Being prepared for any number of possibilities can make a huge difference. I hope that my experience can provide some help for you while navigating through this quagmire of doubts and anxieties. Perhaps, while reading something funny that I went through, a teensy smile, or even a chuckle will break through your tears. After all, looking back, some things are pretty funny. Grab a pencil to jot down anything you read in the next chapters that you might want to remember, and be sure to consult the checklist included at the end of the book.

Perhaps one particular chapter will feel so familiar that it is not only reassuring, but can provide some measure of relief or offer a suggestion that gives help to you, a loved one, or a concerned support person. Remember, "CANCER CAN BE UGLY—FIGHTERS ARE BEAUTIFUL!!"

Chapter 11

My Very First Time

I had experienced a rare, deep, dreamless slumber, induced most certainly by the sleeping pill I took the night before. I awoke very slowly, emerging from sleep as if trying to rise out of thick, cloying syrup. At last, gently parting sealed eyelids and lifting my heavy head, I arose. I was somewhat disoriented, my heart beating erratically in my chest, while my breathing accelerated, attempting to keep pace. I was anxious, nervous, and excited along with a feeling of anticipation about . . . what? Oh, yes! This day, June 20, 2006, was to be my very first session of chemotherapy. The date had been set some time before, and was finally upon me. (Freudian thought?)

My husband, lover, and best friend flitted nervously about me like a moth around a flame. "It will be fine," I told him. "I just need some time to get prepared for whatever this day will bring." This was my kindest way of saying, "Get lost for a minute, I need some space, but I love you and I am grateful you are here." I took a hot, leisurely shower, after which I slathered my body in my favorite body lotion. My usual ablutions, which included the long-neglected chore of shaving, were completed in readiness for my first time.

Some time ago, there was a book and a movie out about a girl who wears red lipstick to her mastectomy. Anyone in this situation can identify closely with that narrative. Male or female, it is important to keep up your daily regimen. Guys, shave and groom your hair; and, ladies, apply a little make-up, and keeping it simple and comfortable, fix your hair. Go forth feeling like you look your best, and you might actually feel better. Dress for comfort as well. A soft, colorful sweatsuit with elastic waistband and a loose top is one good choice. If you have a port or other venous device, make sure it will be easy to expose, (and not too much of you!) in order to access it for your chemo infusion.

I had several soft, comfy, sweat suits of varying bright colors, which became my chemo clothes exclusively. I even donned tube tops so that exposing my port would not expose me, as well. Don't forget to include nice warm socks or soft slippers, because your feet can get cold and icy during chemotherapy. I always applied a little bit of make-up, just to enhance a natural healthy complexion, and brushed out my long hair, or pulled it back into a clip if it was hot outside (that is, while I HAD hair). A light spritz or splash of a favorite fragrance completed my physical preparations.

Knowing that it would be a long day, I ate a big breakfast. Eggs, toast with our home-grown and canned raspberry jelly, topped off by an aromatic and steaming cup of coffee, completed my "first time" menu. I soon learned that my enjoyment of eating became subject to change at the whims of chemotherapy's "appetite magicians." Amazing how they could make it disappear! (Or, sometimes, change it right before my very eyes.)

From my nursing experiences (though not yet up-close and personal), I knew that chemotherapy patients, as well as those accompanying them on this adventure, became hungry and thirsty during the long hours of infusion. That morning I packed a little soft cooler with the staples of many a good school lunch. Peanut butter and jelly sandwiches, in case I craved sweets, cheese and butter sandwiches, in case I craved salty, along with cookies, fruit, and chips. All these went into the pack, enough for both of us, including bottles of Gatorade. An odd effect of Decadron (more on this wonder-drug later), when added to the chemo mix, is that it may alter the amount required to fill you up. Most facilities provide coffee, tea, and water with vending machines for soda and juice. However, I'd encourage you to pack your own, both to save money and to ensure that your favorite kinds are available for yourself and your caregiver.

By the way, the more fluid you take in the faster you can flush the toxins and destroyed cancer cells out of your body. So, drink, drink, drink! Prior to chemo, while your taste buds are still unaltered, try out various flavors of Gatorade to find the ones you like the most. Assemble a "chemo survival pack" with lip balm (guys too, dry lips are non-gender), hand lotion (the dry thing again), Kleenex, bottled water, lollipops or Lifesavers (you guessed it, dry throat), and a good book or crossword puzzle. Find a small, but roomy tote (one with something on it that makes you smile, such as pictures of your pets, grandchildren, funky flowers, etc.) and load it up. Carry this to all of your chemo treatments, adding or deleting items as you progress along your journey.

This next suggestion came to me from my experience as a pediatric nurse for many years, rather than from any of the doctors. On our pediatric unit, we apply a numbing cream to the littlest (and the biggest) patients before any painful procedures, like a blood-draw or an IV start. About a week prior to my first time, I called my family doctor and asked him to phone into the pharmacy a prescription for EMLA cream. This white cream goes on the skin over the veins that might be used for an IV, or drop a dollop directly onto your port about half an hour before the procedure. The area is then covered with a Tegaderm, a small sticky adhesive square that resembles Saran Wrap. Your doctor can order them, or you can get them where band-aids are sold. The skin under the cream will briefly become numb, which is nice when a needle stick is required. Don't forget to grab a magazine, a book, letters you need to write, or knitting, anything you enjoy doing when you have that rare commodity: free-time! During a chemotherapy session, you will have plenty of it!

Okay, I was now all set to go and really prepared . . . NOT!! There is no way to relieve all the anxieties associated with a "first time" chemo experience, but just try to be optimistic, and think, *This will go well, this will kill the cancer cells.* Expect a new experience of uncharted pathways with many guideposts and assistance to help you along this trip.

Well, we were finally off to my first chemotherapy treatment with both of us alternately quiet or chattering at the same time, feeling our mixed emotions, almost as one. After the infernal, but necessary, paperwork we were ushered through the maze of the treatment center, down a long corridor, to our destination: my chemotherapy administration cubicle. Although it was fresh, clean, and delightfully decorated, just the sight of it triggered a rapid heart rate that I was sure could be heard by anyone next to me. My husband, Bob, seemed to be afflicted with the same runaway heartbeat, as I could feel the pulse in his hand, tightly clenching mine.

At the cubicle I was greeted by a young woman with the dark, empathetic eyes of a doe and a gentle touch to match. At the time I couldn't make out her halo and wings, but they soon became evident. Liz, this newest angel of mine, explained every task she was performing. Once I told her I was a nurse, it seemed she could anticipate my questions and concerns. It was as if an instant bond had formed between us, unspoken but powerfully transmitted. This was the first time my new port would be used, the first time my body would be bombarded by the chemo drug minions, and the first step on my journey in Chemoland. She gently removed the Tegaderm from my port and cleansed away the EMLA cream, then applied an antiseptic so the area would be as sterile as possible. Next, to my great surprise and a delight, she sprayed the area with a topical numbing agent, as well. This little step in my chemo ritual would become more important to me than coffee or chocolate! She sprayed and sprayed until my skin became cold and thoroughly numb. That was great!

Then, with smooth dexterity, she slipped the needle into the port before I really had a chance to get nervous about how it would feel. There was a bit of pressure, and maybe a tiny sting, but just for an instant. It was no big deal! So, ask your oncology nurse to apply a numbing agent prior to treatment, as this really helps. During the actual puncture it may help to think, *Pressure, just pressure,* while you look away. The puncture was a part I did worry about, having handled the special fishhook shaped needle before, and it set up a whole wave of anxiety, but it was really not bad at all. Once your port has been accessed, you can rest easy for a while.

After all the preparations and rushing to get to your appointment on time, you will probably have to wait for your blood results and to be seen by your physician or a highly trained physician assistant (called a P.A.). Your blood will most likely be drawn from your port at the time of access, so there is only one needle stick during each treatment. Next, you will receive a thorough exam to check your vital signs, especially your temperature and blood pressure. The doctor will also review your blood results each time, as some levels could prevent you from receiving chemotherapy. This is an issue which can become a real fear, as nothing will seem as important as completing each chemo on schedule. Fortunately, when blood changes do arise, solutions are often available to fix the problem.

Finally the doctor will proclaim you healthy enough to begin chemotherapy. That pronouncement is the "click of the safety bar over your seat" as you climb back onto your emotional roller coaster. Once I was considered healthy enough to proceed, I was guided back from the doctor's exam area through the maze to my cubicle and recliner. (By the time your chemotherapy regime is completed, you will know that intricate path very well indeed!). Over time, I got a little OCD (obsessive/compulsive) about the way I faced, and would even wait if a recliner facing the direction I needed was not open. (I later discovered that OCD can become very common behavior amongst cancer patients during their chemo.) With so much out of control, it is just nice to be able to exert a little control of your own. Be sure to take the proffered blanket and pillow, or ask for them if they are not offered. Some patients will bring a u-shaped neck pillow for use during their chemotherapy. Make yourself as comfortable as possible.

Once you are settled in, the nurse will hang the first of many bags of IV fluids. These are the support drugs which help in preventing reactions, reducing nausea, and providing replacements for those elements that the chemo thief steals away from you as it charges through your body on its seek-and-destroy mission. Many patients will doze or relax during the administration of these drugs. This is the down time, try to make good use of it.

* * *

Throughout this memoir, whenever possible, I would like to share with you some of the humorous things that happened to me along my journey. Remember, humor is great medicine, even on the chemo unit. Perhaps you may even be able to relate to some of the experiences I will share.

I'll start with a real doozy!

Now I know you remember, I am familiar with some of these drugs and the effects that they typically produce. I had just never been a chemotherapy patient before. The first support drug that they gave me was IV Benadryl. It is administered to help prevent potential allergic reactions. When given orally, it induces sleepiness, and when given IV (intravenously), people usually fall into a deep sleep. That is why you will often see people receiving

IV medications while they are sleeping soundly. They are relaxed and bundled up in their blankets, and may even be snoring.

So, when my first IV Benadryl dose was up and running, I tried to relax. After a short while, I began to experience a very strange sensation. I was starting to feel really funny, odd, that is, not as in HA-HA. As this funny feeling increased, I told my husband, clear as day (in my mind, at least), to "GO AND GET THE NURSE!" At least that is what I heard when I said it. However, he heard, "Geddadurse." Liz came running on the double, but could barely conceal a smile as she explained to me that Benadryl does put most patients to sleep but that it can make others very, very drugged.

It was not long before I really had to use the bathroom. So I got myself up out of the recliner and began to push my IV pole along with me. Suddenly I was yanked back! Duh! I forgot to unplug it from the wall! My husband then unplugged the IV pump and wound up the cord, and I returned to my intended mission. I lurched forward on legs that had turned into Jell-O, and literally bounced off the wall. Bob and Liz hurriedly saved me from myself and, despite my incoherent protests, they walked me to the bathroom. There I insisted I would be fine on my own. Once in side, I literally thunked onto the toilet seat. *Must have just misjudged it*, I thought to myself . . . pretty funny. The whole experience was reminiscent of being very drunk!

The drugged state eventually wore off and nothing else untoward happened (or if it did, I was unaware of it). At some point the drug had its intended effect and I dozed. After about six hours I was finished with the infusions and ready to be attached to a portable chemo-pump for the next forty-eight hours. Not every type of chemotherapy involves the use of a pump, but many do. Both Bob and I were then given excellent instructions regarding the pump and the side effects that might develop. Finally, dazed and still slightly out of it, we were ready to head home. So far, so good. My first chemo session was done, or almost, as I still had to contend with the pump, but at least I could do that from the comfort of my own home.

Chapter 12

A Shocking Revelation!

While Liz was finishing up, flushing my IV port and connecting me to the portable pump, I noticed that Bob was suddenly off and talking. This was quite surprising. The husband I knew was very private, quiet, and even a bit stern. Yet, here he was, transformed into a Cancer Schmoozer. He was joking with the nurses and chatting with any patient who met his eye. He even smiled warmly at everyone.

I wondered what was happening. Perhaps he was just bonding? Or maybe his anxieties and fears were finally relenting? Now that chemo number one was officially on board, he might just be unwinding. Prior to that first chemo, I was wound as tightly as a cobra ready to strike. Neither of us knew what to expect, but I had anticipated the worst. Regardless, be prepared for stress to elicit some different reactions in yourself and in those who love you.

* * *

At long last my first chemotherapy session drew to a close. Rising on still wobbly legs, I had a headache, a stiff neck, and a bit of nausea. However, most of these symptoms were minor, as they had given me medications to help with all that. *This is surely manageable*, I thought to myself with a slight congratulatory smile. By the end of our six-hour, first day of chemotherapy, I wasn't too much the worse for the wear and tear, and we were more than ready to go home.

My pump was slung over my shoulder and calibrated to deliver a small, constant dose of a very powerful chemotherapy agent over the next forty-eight hours. The pump itself was the size of a paperback book, with a carrying case. Its steady, whirr, pause, whirr, pause, provided reassurance that it was working (at least it did during the daylight hours). It would continue running non-stop, twenty-four hours a day, over the next two days. The function of this pump was essential to my particular chemotherapy regimen, so much so that at every visit a brand new set of batteries was installed.

One of the drugs in my personal cocktail, Oxaliplatin, can create a unique set of side-effects. It attacks the nerve endings in the fingertips, toes, tongue, and mouth. Touching anything cold could trigger a very bizarre response. The slightest contact with an ice cube, for example, would set off a dramatic reaction. As a chemo patient receiving Oxaliplatin, I was given a special kit with a pair of neoprene gloves in it. *How silly*, I foolishly thought, *it's still summer.*

However, I soon learned better. The effects of this chemo are so intense that it is highly recommended you serve food and drinks at room temperature to avoid this particular reaction. You may think of summer as a time for ice cream, iced tea, and other cold treats. Well, don't worry about missing these delights because you probably won't even be able to recognize your favorite flavors, much less like them, or even tolerate them.

With all this information stored deep in my newly chemo-immersed brain cells, the one thing I distinctly recalled was that a chemotherapy patient must keep hydrated to help remove the chemicals and flush out the toxins. It was a rather warm day for early summer, so as soon as we got in the door I headed straight to the fridge for a nice cold drink. "Just what the doctor ordered," I jokingly remarked to Bob, adding, "I probably have plenty of time before the Oxaliplatin reaction sets in."

Still a bit woozy, yet functional, I reached into the icemaker for an ice cube. Well, it felt like I had grabbed a live electrical wire! Dropping the cube, screeching and dancing around the kitchen, hands flapping and pump thumping, I must have been quite a sight! "This is just not possible," I yelped. "I can't have a reaction so soon. It must all be in my mind," I proclaimed as I madly thrust my other hand into the icemaker. (Yes, I can be stubborn!) This time, I encountered the searing sensation of venomous snakes sending their poison up my entire arm.

Well, this last effort confirmed it: a reaction to Oxaliplatin comes on fast, and is quite intense. Get help if you need to handle cold food or drinks. If you do not have anyone around to help, use the gloves provided or a pair of heavy rubber kitchen gloves. Keep them right by the refrigerator so you can handle all those cool, refreshing items that you will now have to set out to warm up!

About now I seemed to be engulfed by a Tsunami of fatigue, launched by chemotherapy and its drugs. Chemotherapy is a real walking contradiction—doing well, while being poisoned. As the evening wore on, even speech seemed to require too much of an effort; unbelievable for such a verbal person like me. The day passed me by while vivid images flashed before my eyes and the pump metered out its poison.

Later that evening, a delicious smell floated into my nostrils and gently nudged me awake. What could be better than a homemade grilled cheese sandwich and a bowl of soup? What a great guy I've got! That modest meal not only sustained me, but really hit the spot. To insure a good night's sleep, I took a prescription sleeping pill. The pump on my nightstand had a rhythm of its own and I kept unconsciously listening for it, fearful it would stop, much like the mother of a newborn listens for her sleeping infant. I had a fish-hook shaped needle protruding from my chest, about six feet of tubing leading from that to the pump and a large jug of water I knew I should be drinking. Somehow, the reservoir of drugs and the complete mental and physical exhaustion of the first chemo session lulled me into refuge in deep sleep.

Very early the next morning I mumbled to my husband that I was fine, though a little tired, and I encouraged him to go to work. He set some things next to me, brushed a kiss lightly on my lips and I slithered back into my dark, dense oblivion.

Much later that morning I found that I couldn't get up! Really! I just could not wake up. My eyelids felt glued shut, and as I tried to peer out I could only see the red and gold sparkled filmstrip that runs across the inside of one's closed eyelids. With a great deal of effort, and what seemed like the crackle and pop of opening a paint-sealed window, I gradually, and oh so slowly, opened my eyes. My world seemed familiar, and yet alien at the same time. The assault of the chemo on my brain and nerve endings was still fresh, and my body had not acclimated to their presence yet.

Suddenly, the covers, so light and comforting the night before, weighed a ton and seemed to be smashing me down. Fighting an overwhelming rush of panic, I shoved the offending covers off with my arms and attempted to swing my legs out from beneath them and over the side of the bed. Surely heavy anchors held them in place. They were utterly immovable. I felt a lot like I imagine a paralyzed person might feel. My head, as I tried to lift it up off the pillow, was a large weighted ball tethered to a fragile stalk. My neck seemed too frail to support its load.

After numerous attempts, I was finally able to sit up and manually push my legs over the edge of the bed. I felt super-drugged, as indeed I was. Though still foggy and lethargic, it became evident that I desperately needed to negotiate the short distance from our bed to the bathroom. This enterprise was similar to those following youthful indulgences, including the unsteady gait and random bounces off furniture and walls. The end result was a loud thump as my bottom hit the toilet seat, when my chemo-laden leg muscles abandoned their task.

Somehow, my body remembered why it was there and thankfully cooperated. All that now remained was for me to figure out how to get back to my bed, that beckoning haven which loomed so far away. Clinging to the pump to hold it steady, I cautiously made my way back to the bed where I collapsed in a drugged sleep until almost two o'clock that afternoon. My clairvoyant husband (I can't praise him enough) had left me Gatorade, water, and snacks at my bedside to tide me over until these feelings subsided.

From this experience, I now know the importance of having your caregiver set you up with easy-to-reach light snacks. Crackers, fruit, or toast are good options. Most importantly, prepare a jug or thermos with room temperature (no ice!) drinks that you know you can tolerate. Water is good, but due to the propensity of chemotherapy to rob your body of certain elements, Gatorade, or some other enriched beverage, is better. You probably will not be able to drink cold products, so these items can be set by your bed the night before.

I discovered that being prepared seemed to help alleviate some anxiety. If your first morning, post-chemotherapy, finds you feeling exhausted, you probably are! Just go back to bed and allow the drugs to leave your body. Drinking helps move things along, but just resting works wonders. I later learned that this phenomenon is reported by many cancer patients after receiving chemotherapy. For some, it occurs only the first time, but for others it may continue throughout the course of their chemotherapy.

Regardless, it is important to remember that *this too shall pass,* and *when you can do, you will do.* That became my personal anthem, *When I can, I will . . .* I softly intoned this anthem to myself daily to help me forgive my inabilities, and to encourage my possibilities.

At last, the dawning of the third and final morning of the pump arrived. After looking at the glowing numbers every hour for the last few hours, it now appeared to be almost empty. I was pretty confident that I wouldn't be able to drive (duh! I could barely walk!), so I arranged for one of my angels and dearest friend, Patti, to take me to have my pump disconnected. We planned to get breakfast while waiting for the snail-paced pump to finish its job. I even suggested we go shopping after I got unplugged. Wow! Talk about trying to maintain normalcy. That idea would turn out to be unrealistic at best.

We all know about those best laid plans of mice and men . . . I guess that would include women, too, especially those getting chemo for the first time.

It gets worse, though I had no idea.

I made an appointment with my nail tech and friend to get a manicure while waiting for the pump to meter out its final cc's. Getting my nails done was such a routine activity, that I never thought beyond the moment. Patti sat patiently by while I got my nails decorated. I was grateful, as I sure couldn't decorate my life at the time. They were now a beautiful shade of pink with a splash of summer flowers painted on for fun, and because that is what I do. I always had art at my fingertips, so to speak. (Thanks, Kath!)

After this, we went straight to the local diner where Patti, my pump, and I had breakfast. Just as we finished (thankfully I could still eat with gusto), the alarm on the pump heralded the good news: I was just about done! With only a very few drops of the precious 5F-U remaining (a cancer drug geared to treat the bowel), we sped down the road to the oncology center, about five minutes away. The final steps were completed gently and professionally by Liz, my chemo angel. She pushed, (that means squirted with a syringe) the remaining few drops of the drug into my port, and completed all the complicated and necessary flushing to prevent clotting of the port. Then, she disengaged my fishhook before I even realized she was doing it. Whew! At last that was over. I felt a slight wooziness, but I wasn't driving, so off we went with chemo number 1 completed.

No sooner did we start down the road when a strange and insistent rumbling and gurgling began to churn in my belly. There was no pain or other warning, but suddenly, there was an intense pressure right where I was sitting. That meant only one thing, I NEEDED A BATHROOM, STAT! I quickly informed Patti of my impending doom and, being a nurse as well, we both realized this was a force greater than either of us. Certain that I could not make it home, I realized that we were right by Kathy B's (my nail salon and friend). I desperately shrieked, "Turn, turn, and floor it!!"

As we screeched into her driveway I leaped from the car with one hand tightly squeezing my butt cheeks together, while I clenched those muscles firmly and attempted a deep breathing exercise. I raced through her shop yelling, "It's not a nail emergency, it's a bathroom one!" Finally I reappeared with a sense of unsurpassed relief. Kathy's bewildered expression diminished as I told her how she'd just saved me from a chemo catastrophe. I further explained that I must have developed some side effects from that last "push" of my chemo, just minutes before.

Patti, ever concerned, asked if she should take me right home. Now, here is where a little knowledge can go a long way. "No way," I told her, "I am doing fine! Let's go shopping." A few minutes later we were back on the road, but thankfully not yet past the road back to my house, when the feeling began again. By now I was beginning to understand—chemo controls some things, not you. Once again I tried to make Patti into an Indy driver and begged, "Faster! Hurry Patti, gun it!" She barely had time to hit the brakes in my driveway when I flew out the door yelling my goodbyes and apologies, all the while racing into the house.

I barely made it to that most welcoming sight, my toilet. There have been days since, with my stomach roiling like a ship tossed on a hurricane-buffeted sea, when I DID NOT! While on chemo, Imodium (an anti-diarrhea medication) might become your new best friend. Take it with you . . . everywhere. Some days might have to start with it. Be sure to ask your oncologist for a "diarrhea protocol"; a medication plan to prevent or slow down the devastating affects of diarrhea. The true moral to this little story is: do not plan to go out to eat, get your nails done, and go shopping the very first time you complete your course of chemotherapy, unless, of course, you have a port-a-potty in your car.

Chapter 13

Fourth of July—No Fireworks, Only Waterworks

Monday, July 3, marked my second chemotherapy treatment and I approached it with much less anxiety. My mindset was centered on a perpetual countdown, so I was more than ready to have chemo number two under my belt, thus lowering the remaining number of treatments to ten. The day seemed just about right as we departed bright and early to begin the next leg of our journey. We were ushered on our way that morning by a brilliant blue summertime sky accentuated with a few cottony clouds that seemed to emphasize its azure depth, and reaffirm my lust for life.

Upon our arrival, we began what was soon to become a familiar routine. First, Liz would access the port and then withdraw numerous tubes of blood. That blood would be tested to confirm that all the values were at a satisfactory level to receive the toxic load that would be monopolizing the bloodstream. Next came the infernal waiting to be seen by the doctor who, hopefully, would decree me fit enough to be a chemo recipient during that visit. Finally, there was the flood of relief when you are deemed worthy to go ahead. (Many factors could actually postpone the administration of your chemotherapy, more information on this will be provided later.)

I found just the right cubicle, with a lounger facing the direction that my Feng Shui indicated I needed, and Liz was there to begin my IV drip. She expertly administered the support medications, and I had only minimal side effects at that time. It was a long day—9:00 a.m. to 3:00 p.m.—but, *one more down*, I thought to myself, as Liz finally primed and connected the pump, readying me to return home. We stepped outside, my pump and I, feeling my now familiar double W's, (weak and woozy), but still holding my own. My husband needed to make a quick stop at the local hardware store, but planned to go out of his way to take me home first. "Oh, no!" I protested. An outing, however brief, would afford me fresh air to breathe and a car seat to sit on rather than the couch. I begged him to go directly to the hardware store or, in the language of Monopoly, to pass GO, and not stop at my jail just yet! He reluctantly acquiesced.

I savored the sights and sounds of the outdoors, and even the music on the radio seemed special, just for me. Too soon, my wonderful mini field trip was over, and the feelings associated with poisoning descended upon me as the pump continued to meter it out. We returned home and I resumed my position on the couch, with the pump on the TV table by my side. That clever little table would become an addition to our family room furniture, for the next year.

Oddly enough, my favorite foods seemed tainted. During my post-operative periods at home (before chemo) I loved canned peaches and cottage cheese. They are good for you, as the healing body requires greater amounts of calcium. Tasting them now, however, evoked a very definite "Yuck!" they seemed to have turned bad! I made poor Bob my taste tester. He quickly polished them off, saying they were "fine, good, actually." Yet again it was just the chemo burglars stealing away my capacity to taste. My hips and back were achy, I had a bit of a headache and, of course, diarrhea. I was whipped! So, I took my meds and drank some Gatorade. I could only tolerate the taste of the orange version, even though Bob brought just about every flavor they made. Soon I fell into a delirium and rested sporadically as best as I could.

My snooze, which tuned into a three-hour sleep, was terminated by Bob's latest culinary presentation. Toast and scrambled eggs fit the bill perfectly, and, to my surprise, they really tasted great. Per chemo's dictates, I dozed the rest of the evening away. As night approached, we changed venues and headed up to bed. Bob's arm firmly around me was very much appreciated, as those steps sure seemed steeper than they had been that morning.

The shrill ringing of the phone split the evening's serenity just as I was beginning to relax in my bed. Ever wary of the needle, and its partner in crime, the pump, I reached out carefully to answer it. Sensing it might be my son Zack, a smile spontaneously lit my face. His calls filled me with joy like a ray of sunshine splits a stormy sky. It was indeed Zack, but he had devastating news. He and his fiancé had broken up! "Mom, she is leaving!" he said, as his plaintive words tumbled out in a torrent, ensnaring my heart as well. I forgot about my chemo, my pump, my cancer—EVERYTHING, but my son. I was hopeful, trying to console and encourage. "Sometimes things look better in the morning" I tentatively suggested. Her parents were in Florida for a visit and, aside from the petty annoyances arising from cohabitation, homesickness had filled his fiancé's entire being. It seemed she just had to go home and be with her family.

Zack and I talked at length, trying to make sense out of things. Finally it seemed he just couldn't squeeze out one more word. A combination of utter sadness and total helplessness made for bad bed companions that night, forget about the fishhook, and pump . . . The next morning's news completely punctured my heart. She was indeed packing up her things and moving home with her parents. My feelings alternated between profound unhappiness and anger. I was angry that my son would be left alone in Florida while she stole away with her parents.

Stress rarely helps us, especially in matters of chemotherapy, but it was unavoidable now. My stomach rolled and my guts raged in perfect synchrony with my emotional upheavals. Every time I thought of my son and his predicament, my eyes filled with tears, my guts clenched, and my emotions bombed. I think I actually suffered as much as he did.

Fortunately, youth is resilient. Thank goodness my brother, Stu, lived close to Zack. He was a godsend, and he acted like an extension of me, taking Zack out with his family on their boat. While it could not entirely alleviate his sadness, at least he was not alone on the Fourth of July holiday. My husband and I really wanted to see him, and we agreed that it might not be a bad idea for him to come home for a visit, as well. Soon it was all set. Zack would be coming home on July 21, after I received chemo number three on July 18. What an incentive to get myself together this time. "Where there's a will, there's a way!" was now my new mantra.

For three days after my third chemotherapy treatment I was hounded by the "weak and woozy twins," as they just would not leave me alone. Finally, I got the pump unplugged and managed to clean the house up a little bit, sleep a lot, cook a few things, rest, bake, and doze—all interspersed with frequent visits to the bathroom. I was exhausted but exhilarated by the time Bob came by to get me, to go and pick up Zack on the 21st. Everything was ready, his room fresh and clean, and his favorite goodies had been prepared. I could not believe I did it, chemo and all!

It was a salve to my soul, having Zack home during that week, and all my problems were shelved during that time. I planned and prepared a small picnic for our family and a few friends. Bob and Zack helped so much, doing many of those things I usually did in preparation for a picnic, before my chemo regime. Zack put the tables in place, opened the umbrella, and got the drinks on ice (though not mine!), while Bob manned the grill. Our neighbors, Vince and Marie, came over, toting her famous potato salad. Bob's cousins, Karen and Johnny, and their two daughters, long time special friends of Zack's, arrived with a contribution of sweet treats.

While small and simple, it was an unbelievable feat of extraordinary strength for me, given that I was on chemo! Who would have thought that performing such a mundane task would fill me with such a sense of accomplishment? This was, in reality, a very low key and modest affair, compared to my usual entertaining, but it ranked pretty high on my current chart. Being around the girls was good medicine for Zack, and they even coaxed a few laughs out of him.

In the days that followed, we continued to thoroughly enjoy each other's company. In the evenings, after Zack returned home from fishing or looking up old friends, we often just chilled out, feeling completely relaxed. His presence was a comfort to me, and I hoped being home provided him with solace and comfort as well. We would talk long into the night, often after Bob went up to bed. "Waterworks" were our common denominator, mostly from me, given my fragile emotional state. In our own ways we each fortified and comforted the other—often with no words, so strong was our bond.

The week flew by, and driving Zack to the airport was bittersweet. I knew how much I would miss him, but the time we shared was mutually beneficial. The maternal-child bond generated a healing balm that soothed each of our broken parts—body and heart, respectively. He wanted his mom well and healed, and I wanted him well and healed, and his spirit restored. Bob and I both worried about his emotional, and physical well being. However, as parents we could only do so much; he had to do the rest.

Thankfully, Zack and I remained in constant telephone contact during my entire chemotherapy program despite, or perhaps, because of his own dilemma. His brother Jeremy, who had always kept frequent tabs on my progress, now maintained a lifeline for Zack, as well.

Chapter 14

Sex on Chemo?

Ladies of my reading group, read on—no thrusting . . . !

During that first round of chemotherapy my body defied the drugs provided to put me to sleep. Instead of inducing restful slumber, they merely swathed my brain in cobwebs. Once home, events of that first time played out like old re-runs, repeating over and over in my mind while I lay around, feeling like little more than a receptacle for my miracle potions. Without my nurse and hubby at my side, I obsessed about the wisdom of getting up and moving around, knowing that the drugs would alter my memory and judgment. I particularly worried about the umbilical relationship with my chemo pump, and the consequences that forgetting it and jumping up would incur.

While receiving my first chemo, it must have been quite comical when I leaped up and marched forward, only to be pulled up short when the pump I was pushing reached the end of its cord. Then, however, my ever-vigilant husband and nurse were instantly on me like magnets, righting my wrongs. I recalled bouncing off the walls (literally) when I tried to walk in my drug-intoxicated state, which I thought was hilarious at the time. Kindly, they did not laugh as I shrugged their supporting hands off like a cheap coat and forged ahead on my own. I was like a pinball, shot out of the slot onto the flippers, as I ricocheted from wall to wall. In a quasi-drunken state, I was nevertheless guided and supported by my husband's strong arms, girding me up even as I fought for independence. That strength took on a very alluring appeal as I finally, but fitfully, dozed.

***

During a subsequent chemotherapy session I managed to ride the wave of drugs in better form, actually dozing during the Benadryl administration. Not so, this time, however. The chattering of my teeth, rat-a-tatted along my skull bones and awoke me with a start. I found myself enveloped in unimaginable cold, and it seemed like liquid ice had replaced the once warm blood flowing in my veins. My core temperature felt like it was plummeting rapidly. Even covered parts of my body were cold and trembling. Layers of blankets, my own fleece jacket, and hot tea did little to help control my quaking.

Oddly enough, the switching of IV drugs seemed to induce a thaw, which gradually turned into warmth. Snakelike, I writhed and twisted and began shedding my extra layers. My face turned warm and then hot. Soon I was flushed, my whole body felt hot everywhere . . . Decadron (a wondrous steroid) was now coursing through my veins, leaving my palms moist and my face glowing incandescently. The hair along my face and neck became damp and I developed an unquenchable thirst. Water, Gatorade, or soda, it didn't matter as I just couldn't get enough! Suddenly I was also starving. Unzipping my cooler and digging in, I demolished a sandwich, a container of fruit, a banana, and cookies and chips . . . I was an eating machine!

All my senses soon seemed heightened. The faint scent of my own body lotion seemed to grow stronger and heavier, though not at all unpleasant. I could smell the fragrances on female patients in other cubicles. My husband's aftershave (an old, crisp, spicy standard) suddenly seemed incredibly sexy. I called to him softly and then beckoned him over to me. Clutching his face between my hands, I pulled him in and kissed him repeatedly. He smiled and patted me on the back. "I am glad you are feeling better" was his only response to my ardent behavior. I then went on and on about how strong and handsome he was, and he asked if I was still feeling drugged and confused. "NO" I almost shouted, "I just love you so much!"

"And I love you too" he replied, as he patted me on the back, much as a parent would to calm a toddler.

I kept stroking his arm and touching his face. At some point I think it became annoying, as he eventually said that he needed to stretch his legs and left my side for a while. I could hear him chatting with other chemo patients—men and women alike—as he walked through the unit. He seemed friendly and interested as he shared information and tips, while their shared smiles forged a common bond between caregivers and cancer patients.

This treatment ended later than the others, perhaps due to a delayed start or else the need for additional drugs. I felt tired, but that was not unusual. However, there was something else I was feeling that eluded my full awareness at the time. After we ate dinner (sheesh, more food?), my husband professed that he was tired too. Chemotherapy can be exhausting for all involved. Soon we began to follow our new ritual as we prepared to retire. It included bringing an insulated jug of water, a bottle of Gatorade, and any medications I might need up to the bedroom. Once there, I was connected to the pump that rested on my bedside table, reigning over all as it whirred and paused, doing its chemo thing.

Finally, with all preparations complete, I carefully curled myself into the protective warmth of my husband's body as he spooned against me. This lulled me into drowsiness—not sleep, really, but a semi-somnolent state which seemed to suspend time. Gradually my body became suffused with an odd heat. My heart was pumping, the pump was pumping, and my skin became sensitive and responsive. Softly, gentle hands stroked my back, side, and hips, drawing them in closer, skin to skin, as one organism. My hips took on a life of their own. Slowly they began a subtle rocking motion, coercing my husband's involuntary response. I reveled in the glorious strength and heat we emitted and became aware of an increasing throbbing sensation along all my nerve endings. Its strongest focus was in the tiny bud of my core, which had remained dormant all through surgery and recovery, and up until now during chemotherapy. A swelling, pulsing filled it. Our bodies were slowly awakening from their long, stress-induced slumber. The incessant throbbing between my thighs generated liquid warmth and I pressed back against my husband to engulf him as well.

Ever mindful of the pump, the needle, and the recent surgery, we maneuvered into a ballet of gentle grace and mutual need. Our legs scissored together allowing intimate contact of our most demanding body parts without disrupting a thing. We entwined our arms around each other kissing over and over, gently at first, then deeper and more passionately, each of us feeling grateful for the other, and for normalcy and life itself. Then we felt only each other and our immediate need. Our dance quickened and built to a crescendo, ending with a shuddering release. Peace then covered us like a blanket. We finally slept, wrapped in each other's arms.

Later, we couldn't believe that it had actually happened. Not that it would be such a strange occurrence for us, but the circumstances were certainly anything but typical. Blame it on the high doses of Decadron, or the Benadryl, or any of the array of other drugs, but to me it was symbolic of a resurgence of life and commitment. No matter how briefly we touched, this experience forged our bond of love into something even stronger, unbending, and constant through this time of uncertainty. While I realize this may be the furthest thing from either partner's thoughts, there can be occasions when desire overwhelms us and shuts out our fears. If it is mutual, and feasible, using care and common sense, this very act can release hormones that relax and provide a sense of well being. Imagination and creativity can help overcome some of the obstacles that surgery and chemotherapy may present to block your path. (Pillows can be very helpful, too.)

Sometimes just a shoulder to lean on or a gentle back rub (or rubbing a foot or a leg) can be a most intimate and satisfying activity between two partners. As long as your doctor has not set any limitations regarding sexual activity, and if you are feeling okay when the mood comes over you both, sex can still happen—even during chemotherapy. It is also emotionally therapeutic, as the chemo recipient can actually reverse roles and become a caregiver of sorts, providing solace and comfort to the one who has been caring for them. You may prefer to wait until the pump is finished and removed. But, if the moment is right, then strike while the iron is hot . . . just do it with caution. Remember, this is nature's wonderful gift, and it can be mutually pleasing and beneficial to both participants.

Chapter 15

The Dog Days of Diarrhea

With chemotherapy in the driver's seat, your intestines are in for an experience more erratic than Mr. Toad's Wild Ride—totally out of control. After my first chemotherapy treatment, diarrhea raged through me like floodwaters flashing through a narrow canyon. Having weathered that first chemotherapy, I now felt that I could handle anything . . . intestinally, any way.

Preparedness is the essence of chemotherapy management, so anyone going through such an experience must become well prepared. Soft toilet seats not only offer a nice decorator touch, but they are a real necessity if you intend to spend any length of time perched atop your porcelain throne. Once I might have searched for the perfect padded bra-now, but now I must search even more diligently for the perfect padded seat. Stock up on ultra-soft two-ply toilet tissue, along with economy-sized personal wet wipes (the gentle ones with no alcohol). Get some small traveling packs, as well, to keep in your pocket or purse.

When chemotherapy is directed at the colon and small intestines, it causes the healthy cells lining them to slough off (i.e., shed rapidly) which then contributes substantially to diarrhea. So, whenever "a sloughing you must go," just ensure you do it with quality supplies in hand. Follow your Oncologist's protocol for diarrhea. Take Imodium (or Lomotil, or your doctor's choice) right away and continue using it according to the instructions. It may be needed as frequently as every two hours, until a formed stool is achieved. Carry that little bottle of pills with you like an amulet.

During this time, I had several pairs of lovely Victoria Secret undies that our dog, Mookie, had craftily sneaked out of the clean laundry and gnawed, creating little holes here and there. With the damage already done, I reserved those for my chemotherapy days. On a day, more than a week after my chemotherapy, I bravely ventured out to a movie with a few very close friends. I swallowed an Imodium and then popped the rest into my purse. So, you see, I was prepared.

Arriving at the theater, we found ourselves in a long line queued to see the season's most popular chick-flick. As we finally reached the ticket booth, with just minutes left before the start of the movie, we dug madly into our purses for the requisite money. Whoosh! Out of my purse flew a slip of hot pink fabric, which landed on my girlfriend's arm. "Oops," I said laughingly, "don't worry; they are my clean spares . . ." That actually happened! But having a spare was like having money in the bank. (I eventually added a zip-lock baggie in the event I would ever need to switch).

Sometimes that odd gurgling, followed by a sloshing deep in the innards and an incessant pressure between your butt cheeks, may be the only warning signs you'll get. You will soon come to recognize this as a truly imminent signal of your need for a bathroom. Provided one is available just minutes away, you will be okay. I have sometimes had to run to any available throne I could find, while unceremoniously using one hand to manually compress my buttocks together (and even adding mental images in an attempt to assert control), so urgent can be that need. What a great isometric gluteal muscle toner! Regardless, time remains of the essence, as an ominous gurgling can quickly erupt with the force of Vesuvius, and no manner of manual or mental effort can hold it back.

Little wonder that I eventually became absorbed in Depends commercials . . . It sometimes seemed as if my body was weeping for my once-intact self.

During chemotherapy, as fluids ran from my bowels they also leaked constantly from my nostrils, a phenomenon called *mucositis*. I found it quite disconcerting to be talking to someone (my nail tech, or the lady at the bank), only to suddenly discover that my nose had seeped. Even so, I was just grateful that the seepage was at that end, and not the other. There is a little gauze dressing that I have used with patients recovering from sinus surgery. It resembles a tiny hammock that hooks over both ears and runs beneath the nose, and is called a Dale Nasal Dressing Holder. I sure could have used one to manage my "drippy faucets" (and perhaps other agendas, as well).

Constant liquid stools really wreak havoc on the tender anal area. Chemotherapy can break down mucous membranes and cause inflammation, redness, and, in turn, a very sore ass. Sometimes it felt like I had just slid down a sandpapered banister. Upon inspection (don't ask, but hand mirrors and gyrations come into play), there was a red donut ring; think of those attractive baboons with their similar trademark . . . This may be a side effect of chemotherapy. While temporary, it can be very painful if not properly addressed. In a pinch, apply of a small amount of a diaper rash ointment like Desitin, which can provide some immediate relief. Also, ask your oncologist to write a prescription for a tube of Proctozone HC Cream. It is an odorless, white cream that works like magic—and more important to me, at the time, than my face cream.

Just after my third chemotherapy session I convinced Bob that I could manage just fine on my own, so that he could go to work. I nestled in my warm blankets on the couch, while the poisons coursed through me, zapping cells as they performed their deadly mission. Unfortunately, the aftermath of this treatment caused bedlam in my belly and sludge in my brain. I would only emerge at the whim of my demanding puppy, Mookie, or by order of my bowels. Mookie could sense my situation and would lie beside me with her head resting on my arm and her soulful brown eyes glued to me. She seemed to gear the intensity of her actions to the level of my incapacitation. First, she would start to whimper. If that had no affect on me, she would begin whining, and finally, a desperate, panicked frenzy of barking would ensue. (I surely empathized with her then.) Eventually I guessed that she really needed to go out, and that a bathroom break was in order for me, too.

It was quite a task, in my essentially drugged state, to move at all. "Covers off, feet down, body up, find slippers, shove feet in," and then . . ." ugh . . . stand up. Oh crap! The pump, grab the damn pump! Sheesh!" I had to verbalize each step in order to perform even the simplest activities. "Open the door into the garage, grab the leash, click it onto her collar, hold the pump, hold the pump, open the back door, and step down, carefully." My narrative was always much the same. "Hurry, Mookie, hurry," I begged. My world was spinning, I really needed to go, but the Mook had other ideas . . . I yanked on her leash to speed her up, and in an instant that shrewd little demon dog backed right out of her collar and bolted away. There I was, tethered to my pump, with the leash just dangling. Holding onto both as if for dear life, I hobbled down the street yelling, "Mookie, Mookie!"

Over a block away I briefly spied the sleek black head of that wily little brat. I was frustrated and miserable but relief flooded over me at the sight of her. She was in a neighbor's garage looking for their Lab puppy, her friend, Tinki. I was sure glad that her master Mike, our neighborhood doc and my constant answer man, was not around to visualize this spectacle. Luckily, I found a stick and held it out to her as if I was going to throw it. She bounded to me for a game of fetch and I snagged her and looped the collar over her head. Somehow I managed without entangling the still-attached leash and my six feet of dangling tubing. She boldly sauntered back with her weak and dizzy mistress in tow, almost as if SHE were bringing ME home.

As the summer progressed, so did the number of chemo treatments I'd completed. I reeled from the side effects for several days after each chemo session, but I tried like crazy to live life to the fullest in between, despite myself.

I belong to a wonderful reading group which I have been part of for quite a few years. All the members were aware of my diagnosis and were very supportive. The meetings were held on the first Friday of each month. This particular meeting fell only one day after my pump came off— definitely poor timing for me. It was held at the lake house of one of our oldest members, and we were going to the club's dining room for a peaceful luncheon on the outdoor deck. Often at such times, after the luncheon was over, our most stimulating and heated book discussions would erupt.

I really wanted to try and be part of this delightful afternoon, even though I had just finished my chemo. Leni, a group member, as well as a neighbor and a dear friend, offered to pick me up and take me with her. She understood that I might not be able to cope with the whole meeting (or, my body might not, I should say). I feel lucky and blessed to have the friends that I do. The prospect of relaxing out over the calm lake was just too enticing to ponder the downside of my most recent chemotherapy.

Although I required a great deal more time those days to get ready, I wanted to embrace summer with all my femininity. Therefore, that day I chose to wear a brand new sheer floaty top of delicate turquoise hues. It had little cap sleeves and a long silky sash to tie into a bow in the back, leaving long streamers hanging down. Wearing it, I felt almost like my old self. It did my heart good to connect with all the ladies again, and learn that I was the recipient of many prayers and good wishes. Considering my situation, and the possibility of a reaction to eating after chemo, I ordered quite modestly—just a fruit plate and some cottage cheese. Surprisingly, I managed to eat a bit and felt okay, aside from my usual post-chemo weakness and perpetual wooziness.

Suddenly, it happened! I felt the now-familiar gurgling turmoil and demanding pressure. Without a word I leaped to my feet and dashed to the ladies' room. Those glutei muscles really gained strength as they held back a mighty surge . . . just barely. Once I'd yanked my undies down and hit the seat, it was almost immediately over. I had made it! I stood up a bit shakily, but feeling so much better, ready to wash and rejoin the group. However, just as I reached back to hit the flush, I realized with complete and utter degradation that I had not entirely escaped unscathed. Those long, lovely sashes . . . Oh yeah, there they were, dangling right in the bowl!

Well, not to be defeated by chemo, I rallied to the cause. After a few power flushes, some serious soap scrubbing at the sink, and a little time under the hand dryer, I was soon back in my seat and listening to next month's selections—with no one the wiser. (Now you all know!)

Chapter 16

The Snake Creeps Up

Dedicated to my brave friend, Karen

My sixtieth birthday had not been celebrated in quite the manner I had anticipated. It was certainly still a big deal, but being sliced, diced, chopped, and rendered helpless flat on my back was not on my personal agenda for that special day. Don't misjudge me, as I do realize that what transpired, surgically and otherwise, saved me. I just thought that I would be celebrating such a big day in a big way . . . oh yeah, I guess I did . . . really big . . . Apparently secret plans for another birthday surprise, that were being organized prior to my own big surprise, had been put on hold. My dear friend, Karen, had something up her sleeve for my sixtieth. Knowing how much I loved spa treatments, she had been planning to take me to a spa located at the tip of a finger lake in upstate New York. Now that my surgery was history, and I was well into my chemotherapy regimen, she called to share her exciting news and to select a date for reservations. "Oh, wow," I said. "That is great, and just what the doctor ordered!" I replied with unbridled excitement. This response slipped easily from me in a forgetful moment of joy.

Almost immediately, however, chemo nudged its nasty snout back into my consciousness, setting off a warning signal and giving me an abrupt reality check. The idea of sharing a room and, worse yet, a bathroom, or riding in a car without one, sent my heart racing. Chemo presented major roadblocks to this otherwise wonderful trip. Even so, the notion of being gently massaged and relaxing under the delicate ministrations of a spa facial was so tempting that I could not resist.

The spa offered specials on Mondays and Tuesdays during the summer, and July 31 marked my fourth chemo treatment. So, we calculated the days to determine the optimal time in my treatment cycle to plan this trip. Because I would be bombarded with my artillery of cancer fighters every other Monday, we settled on Monday, August 7. That would be a week past chemo, at which time I should be feeling the best chemo would permit. So reservations were made and the spa treatments were booked; we were both looking forward to some quality time together and this relaxing trip.

Karen lives about an hour north of me, just across the Pennsylvania border, in Windsor, New York. The famous Mirabeau Spa, our final destination, is located about an hour north of her. This trip, my first independent adventure since being on chemotherapy, would begin on Sunday, August 6. The plan was for me to drive up to Karen's that morning, hang out by the pool, relax, and join her family for a dinner out that night. I would then stay with them overnight to facilitate our early departure the next morning. With our plans made and the reservations confirmed, I only had to get through my chemo and its subsequent side effects before we were to leave. Hopefully, I would be on the down slope of side effects by that time.

Monday, July 31, with treatment number four finally on board, I went home, hooked up to the pump for the fourth time, feeling optimistic and hopeful. I'm sure you recall, bowel targeted chemotherapy works diligently in that area, causing cells to slough off. Millions of cells, healthy as well as diseased, break away and are washed out of the body. This process creates turmoil in the intestines, producing sudden bouts of diarrhea and generating copious amounts of noxious fumes. These gasses continue to build up, filling the intestines causing visible distention. Eventually it works its way through the intestines until it finally and mightily, exits the body. At this point, my chemotherapy regimen thoroughly tortured my intestines, but, Hell, that seemed a small price to pay for longevity.

By day three on the pump, I needed to carefully judge the amount of time it took to get from one location to another, and to pinpoint the closest bathrooms along the way. My sloughing had really begun, and there would be no margin for error. When I finally went to have the pump removed, another straw was piled on this weary camel's back; my white blood cell count had dropped dramatically. A fall in the number of white blood cells often happens during chemotherapy, it was just not what I wanted to deal with, at that time, or anytime.

Now, I would need an injection of a drug called Neulasta to help stimulate the production of white blood cells. As my doctor explained it, there is a lower threshold number at which it is still acceptable to receive chemo, but if your count drops below that value, then the chemo treatments will be cancelled entirely. A cancelled check is one thing, but cancelled chemo is quite another! Just the thought of such a delay certainly challenges one's coping skills! You become so focused during chemotherapy that a cancellation of a single treatment can throw you into a real tailspin. So, if your white blood count (WBC) starts to fall and your doctor recommends an injection of Neulasta or Procrit, to help restore your counts to normal, take it to avoid the dreaded cancelled chemo.

So, I got that nasty little bee sting and went on my not-so-merry way with a myriad of possible side effects flipping before my minds eye like flash cards; burning and inflammation at the injection site, as well as bone pain, chest pain, tingling, shortness of breath, etc, etc. Liz explained that these reactions can take up to forty-eight hours to appear. So, after a few days with no new discernable problems, I let my guard down and assumed I would not experience any side effects from it at all.

Early on Sunday, August 6, I headed up to New York with a feeling of excitement, surging through me. Amazingly, I made the one-hour drive without needing to stop even once! This was a major accomplishment, and it buoyed me with optimism. Our visit was restorative to my soul. However, dinner was a delicate affair for me. I passed up my favorite foods, and any number of yet untried meals, in lieu of a simple standard: plain meatballs and spaghetti with just a little salad . . . and NO WINE (or was that whine?) One's taste is dramatically altered when on chemo, and tolerance for various foods will be determined by trial and error—hopefully, in the privacy of your own home. I soon learned that certain salad dressings might be not on my tolerance list. Since I was already well into the treatment process, I was able to quickly interpret my body's signals and I raced to the lady's room just in the nick of time, yet again.

One of my absolute daily necessities, coffee, had suddenly become a horse of a different color, tasting like a bitter, nasty vile potion. I could not believe that it was intolerable to me. However, we managed to find a poor substitute (tea), and we began our trip. By early Monday morning we were well on our way with the convertible top down, the sun warm on our faces, music blaring, and hearts soaring.

As we headed north to the town of Skaneateles, and the Mirabeau Spa, Karen remained ever attentive to my new needs. She pointed out every possible rest stop along the way, but my body cut me some slack and I managed until we stopped to peek in a little shop in the picturesque town. That was perfect timing, they had a LOVELY ladies room. Soon after, we arrived at the exclusive hotel and spa with its opulent grounds, gardens, lush fishponds, and waterfalls. As we got out of the car with our bags and headed towards the gold and purple canopy, I knew it was time to explain my latest bodily dilemma to Karen. There was no telling when it would happen next, and I needed to give her a little warning of what to expect.

"Karen, my guts start to fill up with gas from the chemo," I blurted out. "It is so intense you can actually see a raised swelling growing across my stomach, like a snake."

"What happens then?" she inquired in a matter of fact manner. (Technically, this gas fills up the colon, and then travels down the descending colon on its way out of the body.)

"Well, then I usually get a quick sharp pain and then it comes out."

"Okay," she said, "just let me know when that happens." We talked about how I could actually do that, if we weren't alone, and we concocted the phrase, "The snake is creeping up." With that bit of unpleasant business out of the way, we were grandly escorted into the Mirabeau lobby. The doormen were resplendent in their uniforms, complete with gold braid and white gloves. They presented us with flutes of imported bubbly, each with a ripe, perfect strawberry bobbing on the bubbles.

I had not taken a sip of alcohol since I began chemotherapy and I figured one little sip couldn't hurt. Well I sure thought wrong! That sip set my tongue on fire and left my palate burning—it was as though I had a mouthful of rocket fuel! There was no way to gracefully swallow it. Mercifully, there were many large urns with potted palms scattered about . . . yet another bullet dodged. We opened the door to our lovely villa and reeled from shock as our eyes landed on the lone double bed. Normally we would not give it a second thought, as we are as close as sisters, but with my new predicament I was really anxious. Karen called the front desk only to discover that, apologies for the error not withstanding, there were no rooms with two beds left. Upon hearing this, my brave friend, Karen, just smiled and told me not to worry. "You just let me know if the snake creeps up," she said.

Then, we slipped into our bathing suits and set off to find the whirlpool spa. It was fantastic beyond words, a long, meandering free-form lagoon with pulsating jets everywhere. Water gently slid down the smooth rock waterfall, and gorgeous tropical plants thrived in the warm, steamy atmosphere, their fronds dipping low to partially obscure parts of the lagoon. Easing myself down into the alluring water, I felt all my anxiety melting away . . . but suddenly I felt something else as well . . . The snake was creeping up. Thankfully, Karen and I were the only people out in this tropical paradise, and we were isolated by the thick vegetation and hidden by rock formations that further secluded us. The waterfall incessantly babbled behind us while powerful jets pulsed and spurted all around. Karen got out of the water, briskly dried off, and then stretched out on a luxurious lounge.

I lingered, savoring the feel of the powerful jets and something more urgent building up inside me. At last, submerging myself in the gurgling, swirling caldron, I released the "snake," and immediately relief from that awful feeling swept over me. (Fortunately, it is only gas.) Finally, comfortable again, I climbed out and wrapped myself in a thick towel. Karen suddenly turned toward me and grabbed me firmly by the arm. The speed of her movements rather startled me. Then she said, in what seemed to be a barely controlled voice, "Oh my G-D, Franie, there is a Methane gas leak and it's bad. We have to get out of here and call the management!"

"Oh, Karen, it's just me." I responded with relief. Yet my honesty went unheeded. She assured me she knew methane gas when she smelled it and that it couldn't possibly be me.

We hurried to our room to dress for dinner, and I begged her not to call the management just yet, as I was certain of the source. Once inside our room, we got busy with our individual preparations for dinner. While she indulged in a little more champagne (mine!), I indulged in a mad dash to the bathroom, barely making it in time. When I emerged, I must have been shrouded in a cloud of foul vapor. Karen looked up and shrieked, "The methane, it was you!" We both collapsed on the bed in hysterics. Utilizing all the pharmaceuticals at my disposal, with the exception of frequent mad dashes to the closest ladies room, the remainder of our stay went well. (Note: Using the medications prescribed to you for side effects can help you cope and live as normally as possible under abnormal circumstances.)

When our blissful treatments were, sadly for me, completed, we drove back to Karen's house much more relaxed and peaceful. I was renewed in another way, as well. At least, I knew my body's shortcomings, and they did not entirely control me. I had gone to a spa, had a great time, and had thoroughly enjoyed being pampered, despite being on chemotherapy. It definitely takes timing, careful planning, fortitude, and . . . good meds. On my way home from Karen's I reviewed the pleasantries of the trip and did not dwell on the dread of the upcoming Monday.

While driving confidently with the flow of traffic, I became aware of a backup ahead of me. Traffic was slowing down and finally came to a standstill. As I applied the brakes, a jolt of electricity shot across my back and down my right leg. My confident demeanor slowly ebbed as I nervously contemplated my next move. A slight shift in position sent more current down my back. The only possibility that made sense to me was that there must have been an accident involving power lines and my car was stopped on top of them. Adrenaline surged as I recalled those emergency shows on TV with downed electrical wires—surely I needed to get out! Without another wasted moment I pushed the door open and leaped out and away in one fluid movement. This maneuver resulted in a lightening flash of pain, and ended with me sitting down on the blacktop in the middle of the interstate. There did not appear to be any accident or power lines down and the traffic way ahead was beginning to inch forward. *Hmmm*, I wondered as I cautiously climbed back into my car and carefully buckled up, *what the heck is going on with me now?* With mounting apprehension, I put the car into drive and gradually accelerated to merge back into the flow of traffic.

I remained ever vigilant for the shocks, which continued to occur at no particular time and with no apparent provocation. ZAP! Across my back and down my leg it shot again, leaving me shaky and anxious. I was never so grateful to pull into my own driveway, arriving safe and sound. I ran into the house and dropped into the welcoming refuge of my couch.

The shocks persisted to a lesser degree throughout much of the evening. First thing the next morning I called my oncologist and learned that in a few rare cases, individuals may experience shock-like pains from the Neulasta injection. (Oh yeah, there's that rare word again!) It could even simulate a heart attack, as it shifts the bone marrow in the sternum into overdrive. (The sternum is the breastbone, and in it is bone marrow, which is a prime location for white blood cell production.) For some people, the effects of Neulasta stimulating white blood cell production can be very painful, causing shock-like bone pains. This information is good to know in advance, as it just might save you an embarrassing leap from your car as you flee imaginary downed power lines!

Chapter 17

Hitting the Wall

Summer's haze blanketed everything: steamy, vapor-laden air dampened clothes, skin, and moods. It was hazy, hot, and humid in northeast Pennsylvania that August, and the three H's prevailed. People were sweltering and complaining about the heat as they tried to suck in the viscous air. Reporters were harbingers of doom with their predictions of record-breaking temperatures. "Expect 100 degrees and higher" they hawked, creating news. As the day dawned on the morning of chemo number five, the sun, just a mere sliver had already ignited the horizon, its shimmering waves distorting the landscape.

It was a good thing for Bob that the air conditioning at the chemo center was in excellent working order and cranked up. Living in the Endless Mountains we did not have, nor rarely needed, air conditioning in our home. Florida style ceiling fans usually did the trick and kept us comfortable in the past. My treatment went without any major hitches, for once. Perhaps my body was finally getting the hang of it. Before too long, I would be on my way to chemo number six and at the midpoint (at least that was how I viewed it). This chemo brought on a deep bone-chilling freeze, which I naively blamed on the intense air conditioning. Trussed to my pump, I was oblivious to the oxygen draining heat, I just needed to get home and lie down.

Once settled into my niche on the couch, I burrowed under the afghan waiting to thaw out. Bob came in wearing shorts and a perspiration dampened t-shirt, as sweat trickled down his flushed cheeks. "Holy cow" he complained as he switched the ceiling fan to high and pushed open the sliding glass door as far as it would go. "It is hotter than Hell in here, at least a hundred degrees. You must be miserable!" How right he was, I was miserable! My body was wracked by shivering and my teeth chattered incessantly. I was totally oblivious to a hundred degree day, and yet it was normal for a chemo day. In time, the ice flow in my body reverted back to blood flow and I was finally comfortably warm.

Another complication of chemo is that it can knock your body's thermostat off kilter; patients receiving chemotherapy often experience a wide range of temperature fluctuations totally unrelated to the thermometer reading. One of the chemo drugs, Avastin, is also responsible for elevations in blood pressure. It can create quite a problem if it gets too high, as that can cancel your chemotherapy. As I've said before, and I will say again, a cancelled check is bad enough but cancelled chemo is earth shattering!

As you travel through Chemoland, each treatment is a major milestone towards the completion of your journey. If you must skip even one treatment, it erodes your confidence and pushes your goal further away. Before you begin chemotherapy, a mind-set is established, much like that of a marathon runner. You feel as if you must stay the course, no matter what. I was like a racehorse with blinders on, with only the goal immediately ahead visible. Each time I awaited chemotherapy clearance, innumerable worries kept running through my mind like a broken record: *Let the white blood count be high enough, and the blood pressure be low enough . . . high count, low pressure, high count, low pressure . . .* It was like being a pilot in a new aircraft going through the pre-flight checklist without having the controls to regulate anything.

Late in July, just prior to receiving my fourth chemotherapy treatment, my typically low blood pressure had been surprisingly high. I was positive it was just anxiety-induced, as they had moved my chemo angel, Liz, to another facility that morning. That definitely had me upset. Miraculously, I still got my chemo that day, thanks to another drug that assists in lowering the blood pressure and Dr. Heim's aggressive stance against cancer. The headache I always developed from chemo was persistent and pounding after chemo number five. Oddly, my stockpile of pharmaceuticals barely took the edge off and did not take it away. It got worse and worse.

It was as if nasty little gremlins were spelunking in my head, their sharp axes picking the way along my skull bones. They chose a path behind my eyeballs, looping tiny ropes around the nerves there and yanking harder and harder! My head reverberated with the excavation that seemed to be progressing inside. My brain throbbed in sync with my pounding heart. In fact, my whole body seemed to join in the melee. This intensified the feelings of anxiety I already had, making me feel like something was very wrong! I began sorting through possible medical scenarios, and finally realized I just needed to stay still and as calm as I could, which was no easy task. The night passed, but only with the help of serious sleeping medication. With the first streaks of the buttery dawn spreading across the horizon my anxiety seemed to ease a bit; I would soon be able to contact my family doctor. The minute the office opened I was on the doorstep, a pathetic medical beggar, I needed help! They ushered me right in and it was a good thing. My blood pressure was 198/112, which was dangerously high (nearing the stroke zone)! The Avastin drove it up, even as it drove out the enemy. Thankfully, Dr. Ruggiero joined in the battle and determined that I needed to get on an effective medication stat! Now I had to add blood pressure pills to my already loaded pharmaceutical repertoire.

The medication worked fast to reduce my blood pressure, but not without creating other problems. I borrowed my neighbor's automatic blood pressure device and began taking my pressure every morning. Following the readings, I would adjust my medication depending upon the results. Obviously, if it was too low, the dose would be lowered or skipped. Conversely, if the pressure was still high the dose would have to be higher. It was like playing roulette—I wanted only the low numbers. My blood pressure remained inconsistent throughout the remainder of chemotherapy.

Between the chemotherapy and the high blood pressure, something was now causing blurred vision. Geez, this, on top of everything else! So, I had my eyes examined and was quite thrilled to discover I merely needed a new pair of prescription glasses—finally, something that was just a normal occurrence of daily living! During chemotherapy, it seemed that nothing was 'just normal.' Utilizing frequent bathroom stops, I managed to get downtown and pick out a new pair of glasses (not an easy decision for me in the best of times). They were quite costly, not just because I got all the bells and whistles, but due to my very complicated prescription. I had ordered them out of necessity but now I looked forward to the luxury of a new look, as well as clear vision. It was an especially critical factor for me because I am glasses dependent, and unable to function without them for more than a few minutes. They are always glued to my face, and I have fallen asleep in them and even started to shower with them on. I was excited to finally have a new pair.

Amidst the rigid demands set by my chemo schedule, a visit to Denver to see the kids and their new home was scheduled for August 24, just prior to chemo number six——my half-way mark. As you can imagine, I was very eager to see them, especially with my first grandchild on the way. Even with that enticement, the thought of traveling such a great distance while a chemotherapy patient still triggered scary emotions—indeed they ranked pretty high on my body's Richter scale. This trip would not be without hurdles, and my greatest fear was that my chemo-laden body would betray me. All I wanted was to travel, if not in my normal manner, at least with my dignity intact. I needed to get there without too much discomfort, and then to be able to function with some degree of normalcy.

Aside from the chemotherapy and its complications, I would also have to contend with the effects of very high altitude once in the mile-high city. All of these factors dominated my thoughts as I attempted to regulate my runaway blood pressure. During the next days my blood pressure really fluctuated. One day it was so high I had to take a mega-dose of the medication, the next day it was so low I had to skip it altogether and combat the sudden dizziness accompanying very low blood pressure. (It is common for new-onset of high blood pressure patients to require adjustment of their medications in order to get it under control.)

A few days prior to my own D-day (Denver departure), I was at the kitchen table feeling kind of woozy (nothing new there). It had been a sweltering day and all the windows were wide open. Suddenly, there was a sizzling crackle of nearby lightening, followed instantly by a window-shaking explosion of thunder. Then the sky seemed to open up. I bolted from the table and leaped up the steps to get to the bedroom windows, hoping to outrun the drenching downpour. I am still not exactly sure what happened. (It could have been due to a sudden drop in blood pressure, or perhaps as a result of one of the many drugs onboard). Regardless, I suddenly found myself sprawled on the floor halfway between the top step and the upstairs bathroom. I couldn't see, and my cheek was throbbing. All the while, the rain pelted the curtains and soaked the carpeting . . . WHO CARED!!!

Once my poor addled brain ceased rolling around and ground to a stop, I assessed my situation. Somehow, it seems I must have misjudged the distance and slammed cheek-first into the wall—maybe my pressure had bottomed out. Other than a possible black eye and bruised cheekbone, nothing else seemed damaged. Yet, I still could not see! Panic was creeping up my spine, until it dawned on me that my glasses must have flown off during my ungainly gymnastics. Ah, yes, there they were, on the bathroom floor . . . oh no . . . and in the hallway. Oh my G-D, they were broken— really, really broken!

With that realization, something inside me seemed to snap! There was an unearthly howl followed by unspeakable guttural curses. Minutes passed in utter mindless hysteria, which slowly subsided into sniveling whimpers. I lay there contemplating my fate when I started to wonder, *Where was my knight in shining armor?* He had not come to my rescue, yet . . . Eventually, I gathered my wits, and myself, and collected the pieces of my glasses. The lenses were plastic, so that part was okay, but the frames were in two pieces, and one earpiece had snapped off. I shakily felt my way back downstairs, clinging to the banister for dear life, the windows be damned! As it turns out, Bob was down in the basement with the door closed and never heard a thing.

My ranting and raving turned piteous, and I sat down at the kitchen table once again, now mewling softly. Nothing seemed to matter, just my glasses—MY GLASSES! After what felt like an eternity, Bob opened the door, but my drama, now stale, became his dilemma to fix. All of his MacGyver efforts to temporarily repair my glasses failed, miserably. Hysteria, which had been teetering on the edge, was now creeping closer with each failure. Putting ice to my cheek helped, but I hardly noticed that.

Suddenly, with a shout, Bob emerged from the basement workshop, victorious. In his hands he held a misshapen but whole pair of glasses. I shrieked in joyous relief, flinging my arms around his neck thanking him profusely. Upon closer inspection I began to wonder, *Could they even be worn?* The only way he could attach the delicate pieces and have them hold, was with a hot glue gun. The result was opaque globs of glue at every connection, including one right on the lens, and perched on my nose, they listed at a disturbing angle. Yet, with the somewhat repaired glasses crudely seated on my face I could see, sort of. I was overjoyed with my sanity restored.

The next morning, after a rather crazy and disjointed rendering of the events to another angel (Patty, who works where I got my glasses), I was off, makeshift glasses and all. My unusual combination of astigmatism, near-sightedness, and now, age-induced far-sightedness, has always made getting the exact prescription a difficult process. The irony here is that I would be getting my brand new glasses in about ten days, so I was actually relieved this fiasco happened to my old ones. Under Patty's patient tutelage I was able to find, in their budget department, a very reasonable pair of funky red frames. Just as she had a few days ago with the high-end glasses, she now ordered me generic lenses that would be ready in two days and function just fine. She managed all this with careful regard for my rapidly depleting cash flow, and the end result was actually cute (imagine the talk-show host, Sally Jesse-Raphael, minus the talk show) these would create my smart look. I would be off to Denver in just one more day, but at least I could count on seeing—which was about the only thing I could count on.

Chapter 18

Franie Does Denver

Blood pressure fluctuations and the frequency and consistency of my stool became daily indicators of my well being. I never knew which way the blood pressure elevator would go—up or down? It was a problem I diligently tried to get under control, but, unfortunately, it was under the control of my chemo drug, Avastin. The medication for high blood pressure seemed to help, but the diuretic component of it just added one more stone to my growing sack full of problems to contend with. (A diuretic causes frequent urination.) In an attempt to muster my usually abundant optimism and good spirits, I began to pack for my upcoming trip. According to the weather forecast for Denver, the temperatures over the last few weeks were in the nineties. I saw that as a welcome heat wave to thaw out my chemo-frostbitten soul, and a visit with the kids, just what I needed.

When I was up to it, I packed my suitcase with that in mind. It also resembled a mini medicine cabinet complete with an arsenal of drugs for just about any untoward event. I even filled a prescription of antibiotics from my oncologist and stockpiled a week's supply (a great idea, as a chemo patient becomes immuno-suppressed—which means a drop in the white blood count and a weakened immune system, allowing you to get sick easily.) The altitude at mile-high Denver can affect even the strongest individuals (causing symptoms referred to as Altitude Sickness), and there was no telling what it might do to a chemotherapy patient. Staying hydrated is extremely important while on chemo, but at high altitudes it is critical for everyone. So, I packed a carry-on bag with travel-approved snacks and a water bottle to sip before entering the secure areas. I was really worried about all the restrictions in air travel since the 9/11 terrorist attacks, coupled with the restrictions already imposed by chemotherapy.

August 24 was an unseasonably cool morning here, so I dressed in jeans and a fleece, ready to tackle Denver. I ate a light, but fortifying, breakfast and swallowed a handful of pills, covering all my bases. Finally, we were off. Although Bob was happy for me to be able to make this trip, he was also torn and fraught with anxiety over my continued well being so far from home. He was visibly anxious as he held me tight and kissed me, reluctant to let go. After a sweet embrace and one last kiss to hold us, Bob walked me to the edge of the security area. He turned and, with an anxious little backwards glance, he left me on my own. I quickly sipped from my water bottle, trying to empty it before it was my turn to go through the security arch and x-ray machine.

Between the various and sundry surgical bric-a-brac in my belly and the recently installed Port-a-Cath in my chest, I anticipated triggering the nerve wracking alarms as I approached the security checkpoints. Before I could set them off, I wisely shared a brief version of my story with every TSA agent I encountered. I was armed with notes from my surgeon and oncologist, just in case. Miraculously, I passed through the screening process without a snag and was even allowed to refill my empty water bottle once I was through to my gate. How fortunate for me that the agent at the gate had recently gone through chemotherapy with his wife, who was now doing well. After a few moments of mutual commiseration, he walked me right into the plane and situated me in a bulkhead seat directly across from the lavatory . . . he may never know what a wonderful thing that was. After this flight, I knew it took exactly fifteen steps from my seat to the restroom, a fact quickly tabulated during my many ventures there. Despite everything, the flight went well. I was excited and looking forward to a relaxing visit in the warm dry air of Denver. Prepared for a solo trek through Denver's labyrinthine airport to the baggage claim area, I was surprised and thrilled to see my tall, handsome son waiting inside the gate just as I stepped off the plane. What a wonderful sight! He, too, is a Special Agent (like Bob), and because of that, he was able to use his badge to gain access and aid his dear old, slightly weak, and altered mom, much to my joy.

My heart surged, puffing up with love for my son. We hugged fiercely and he snatched my luggage from the turnstile then led me out and settled me into his waiting car. There, he instructed me to drink the Gatorade he brought so I would not get an altitude-induced headache. (Wow, a new reason for a headache!) He laughed as he looked me over and said, "Mom, you don't look too bad."

The weather in Denver was delightful—very warm with no humidity—as Jeremy gave me the royal tour of their neighborhood and home. I continued to try and maintain an iota of dignity, even with my body under the influence of chemo, which was a very inconsiderate and inconsistent boss. Nevertheless, the chemo boss would often issue orders, and I would find myself racing up the steps (no easy feat with chemo fatigued muscles) to reach the exalted porcelain throne where I so frequently worshipped. It was wonderful being with them, but I no doubt overworked their bathroom. I constantly cited my chemo as an excuse for my frequent and hasty departures as well as other bodily functions.

They took me to Golden Colorado to tour the famous Coors Brewery, which turned out to be fascinating and a lot of fun. We all got special wristbands that would give us ample opportunity to sample many brews. Remember the affect champagne had on me? Well, no one can accuse me of being a poor sport, as I still tried. Sadly, beer was awful, too, but the company was great. After the tour we drove all the way to the top of Lookout Mountain, just in time to catch the leading edge of a fluke cold front. Dressed for the expected high temperatures, I was buffeted by chilling winds and a temperature drop of almost 40 degrees. Can you believe that dumb front stayed in town as long as I did? So much for my new vacation wardrobe, as I apparently wouldn't need the shorts and tank tops. The jeans I arrived in, and my fleece, became my mainstay.

Luckily, my thoughtful son had mailed me a long-sleeved black shirt bearing the famous logo "Livestrong," as well as the now-familiar yellow cancer awareness wristbands. I was rarely without that touching and warm shirt during the visit. (Bob and I slipped on those wristbands the day they arrived in the mail, and we still never take them off.) Our visit to beautiful downtown Denver was a new experience for me, and very enjoyable. Fortunately, there were many public bathrooms interspersed amongst the unique stores. For any expedition we took, I had to question the distance of the drive and the location of bathrooms along the way. I tried so hard to camouflage my inadequacies and present a normal front (for me, or them, who knows?), but my strength was sapped by the chemo and I was slogging through the thin altitude by sheer willpower. Extreme diarrhea and the possibility of the "snake creeping up" haunted my every moment. Even so, while it was not an easy venture, it was something I needed to do so very much!

On my last night in town I wanted to treat them to a dinner at the place of their choice, which was Asian Fusion. Hmmm, nothing was starred as chemo-friendly, so I ordered carefully, but ended up tolerating only tea and rice. The kids not only enjoyed their dinners but reaped the rewards of my shortcomings. I had my untouched dinner packed up for their next meal at home. We spent a nostalgic night in their beautiful home, and as I put my hands on my daughter-in-law's round belly, I felt my granddaughter's impatient kicks under my palms. No doubt she was just saying, "Hi, Grandma!"

Chapter 19

Not a Cancelled Check?

As summer came sliding toward home plate, chemo was just rounding third base. Fortunately, this was one of those few times that I was blessed with a rare surge of energy. It felt like what I was accustomed to in my old pre-cancer, pre-chemo life. During that brief period, I did everything I could! I cooked, cleaned, shopped, went to movies, Tai Chi, and my reading group. I felt like my internal batteries were placed on a super-charger, producing a real energy burst. Perhaps this was as a result of my recent visits with our distant and much beloved family. Time spent with your grown children is indeed a great blessing.

We take for granted being able to perform the most mundane activities. For someone receiving chemotherapy ordinary tasks require extraordinary efforts. Things like stripping beds, toting laundry down a flight of steps to wash, folding it and climbing back up the steps (nearly spent) to make the bed anew, may be tantamount to an Olympic event. It was not just one day at a time, but one step at a time, sometimes it was an effort to manage even a baby step. Bob became my household shadow dancer. If I tried to do any of these routine chores when he was around, he materialized out of thin air. The laundry basket, sheets, or vacuum, were whipped out of my hands. Completing these acts on my own became a clandestine mission. I know it seems odd now—what woman would not to want help with household drudgery? Yet, a part of my pre-cancer identity was my ability to juggle household chores, work part-time, and maintain a busy social calendar. Thus, when the chemo burglar slipped into my world and robbed me of these simple skills, I relished the days, or even hours, when I was able to reclaim them, even if only temporarily. Even so, when I just could not muster the energy required to perform a chore, Bob's strong arms and unfailing support, household and otherwise, were unbelievably welcomed. However, the sight of the clean, folded laundry or a freshly made bed, the result of my solo efforts, brought me great joy. Of course, after that I would often crash back into bed, exhausted by my efforts, but with a sense of accomplishment none the less.

The day after my return from Denver, my mid-way treatment was scheduled. After its completion, half of this grueling treatment would be completed! In my typical fashion, just to celebrate this momentous occasion, I picked up a few little fun gifts for my medical helpers. As always these days, Bob went along with my silly endeavor and loaded the colorful tissue-filled gift bags into the car. My presence was my gift to him, he often remarked, as there were no bags ear-marked with his name. So, he'd just have to make do with the one he lives with. (Ha, Ha!) That morning I awoke with a rare feeling of elation. The number of treatments remaining would finally be going down now. Oddly enough, though, on the way to the chemo center I was weak and exhausted. *It's just the trip, nothing to worry about*, I mused to myself while waiting for my lab results and medical clearance. After all, traveling while on chemo can wear out any cancer patient. Oddly, the entire time we were waiting, I had to concentrate on holding my head up, and it became a real effort.

I had my legs kicked right out from under me when I heard the results of my pre-chemo blood work. So much for that wonderful feeling. My white blood count was low again—way too low. It meant that the immune cells that help the body fight off infection were not plentiful or even adequate. Chemotherapy can severely slow down production, leaving you vulnerable to the most insignificant of microbes. For a new twist, my once upon a time in the land before chemo low blood pressure, was once again way too high. A serious side effect of Avastin, one of my main chemo drugs, is elevated blood pressure. That is not safe for anyone, on chemo or not.

At the doctor's request, Liz administered Ativan, a drug that helps to reduce anxiety and lower blood pressure, which was apparently to no avail. Both problems remained, and prevented me from receiving chemotherapy for the first time! Yes, this milestone session was cancelled! I begged and cajoled, and even refused to leave until I spoke to the physician on call. Dr. Heim was not there that day and poor, sweet Michele had to drag the other doctor in to deal with me, as I would not budge. He only reinforced the dreaded decree: "It's not safe. No chemo for you today!"

I felt like the chemo Nazi had taken Dr. Heim's place. "Oh, woe is me," I sniveled, suddenly as deflated as a punctured balloon. Eventually, the affects of the Ativan silently kicked in, and I was really whacked out! I felt strangely calm, as all the frustration of my recent cancellation dissipated with the last drop of the drug. Bob suggested we stop at the food store and pick up a few things, as I would not be on chemo for a while and might actually enjoy eating something. Shopping for food was becoming a daily activity, and I would just doze in the car anyway. So, off we went. Believe it or not, we bought a pound of fresh crabmeat and other goodies. After I rested a bit I made crab cakes, creamed spinach, and buttered noodles for our dinner. I not only surprised Bob, but myself as well. With no chemotherapy planned for another week, I ate plenty and actually savored it. Liz also gave me an injection of Neulasta to stimulate my white blood cell production, so I soon had to revert back to my old shelter on the couch with the heating pad cranked up. My belly was pleasantly full but my pleasure was short-lived as I rode the electrical jolts of the Neulasta, repeatedly zapping my back and hip bones.

Surprisingly, I actually developed an appetite and gained some weight back during this enforced reprieve. Chemo number six was rescheduled for the following Tuesday, and my happy little gift bags remained hidden, silently waiting in the back of the car.

When September 5 rolled around it was time to try for chemo again, and I was an emotional yo-yo. My mood would soar one minute and then plummet the next. On my way to the chemo center I told Bob, "Just leave those stupid little gift bags in the car." So, we entered the center empty-handed, with me dragging my moping ass behind me. Amazingly, the numbers were in my favor this time: blood pressure down, white count up. "Houston, it's a go!" I told Liz with a big smile on my face. Bob did his usual disappearing act while Liz accessed my port (the only part he could not bear to watch), and he returned shortly, laden with the goodies from the car. My delight was contagious as everyone opened the bags while the much-awaited chemo cocktail dripped into my bloodstream. "Six down, six to go," I happily chanted, as we left the parking lot for home.

However, chemo session six did not go down so easily. The ever-lurking twins, weakness and wooziness, came for an uninvited visit and brought along their good friend, nausea. Thankfully, my medicinal landlord worked overtime to keep their stay brief, and eventually kicked them out.

We celebrated our twenty-ninth anniversary five days after chemo number six. I dressed up a little bit (still no easy task), and we went out to dinner to celebrate. Normally, we would have shared a carafe of wine. However, for the duration of chemotherapy I could not tolerate even a drop of alcohol—a fact already confirmed by my few attempts. So, we toasted to long life, health, and our love, with iced tea. As our glasses touched, so did our hearts, and Bob said the most beautiful words, causing tears to well up and slide down my cheeks. These were tears of joy at just being able to share this wonderful moment. I could have sworn I saw moisture glistening at the corners of Bob's eyes, too—or maybe it was just the reflection of the candlelight off his glasses?

Chapter 20

Change—and Not Just Pennies and Dimes

At this point in chemotherapy, my entire body was increasingly adversely affected by the absorption of so many toxic chemicals. Some changes were obvious, even to me. Others were more insidious, as they affected my muscles, nerve endings, taste buds, and other previously unsaturated parts. My mouth and tongue became the latest victims of chemo, as I developed excruciating sores. Some were in very odd places. The underside of my tongue would become sore and inflamed to the point where eating anything was agonizing, and even talking was difficult. A particularly frightening symptom was the development of tender swollen glands under my jaw and down my neck. I would obsess about them, and thoughts of *What is it? What caused it?* plagued me until I could reach Michele. She was the voice of reason and sanity in my temporarily insane world. She kindly explained to me that, "the mouth is part of the entire digestive system, and all of the tissues inside, including the tongue, are under assault from the chemo." The painful swellings were most likely related to the sores in my mouth, as they were an integral part of the body's defenses.

Never hesitate to call your health care providers, nurse or PA, or the doctor when you experience any new problem. They need to know about it in order to adjust your medication doses, and they may have solutions to help you cope. In my case, a mouthwash and numbing topical spray were lifesavers. Ask your doctor about Biotin mouthwash and Magic mouth rinse. You can also obtain Chloraseptic spray and lozenges right from the drugstore . . . what wonderful relief.

I have already alluded to the revolt of my taste buds, but by this time I was lucky if anything tasted right. Drinking liquids could be incredibly daunting. Parched from the poisons cursing through my system I might crave a particular drink, only to find that it tasted awful. However, this facet of chemotherapy was inconsistent. I was a big-time coffee lover—not just enjoying the taste, but also the familiar feelings it induced. It was energy in a cup. Perhaps that evolved from the years of nursing in the emergency room when a cup of coffee might have been all I could get for hours on end until a crisis was resolved. That particular love was one of the first sacrifices chemo demanded of me. Things that I previously loved became inedible and vice-versa—all at the whim of taste buds that were really not my buds. You may want to experiment cautiously and then savor something you find pleasant. Enjoy it for as long as you can, as it will probably soon change.

One morning while slicing my breakfast bagel (a great staple for the chemo-challenged), I somehow sliced the inside of my thumb as well. *No biggie, everyone has done that. I was probably just in a hurry*, I thought, silently reassuring myself. From that day on, I paid special attention while cutting things, but it did not seem to improve the situation. Just about daily I sported band-aids on the tender area inside of my thumb. Do you think the clear ones I bought camouflaged my problems? Well, in my mind I guess it did . . . as I kept right on with my prep work—no sous chef for me!

While slicing an onion I literally opened up my thumb, right in front of Bob! That was not good. While applying pressure, I stuttered and stammered but couldn't justify my unusual clumsiness. After careful inspection, I realized it was not a matter of carelessness at all but an issue of loss of feeling in my fingers. All my empty explanations for the frequent cutting accidents, "The knife must have been greasy," or, "I had butter on my fingers . . ." could not sustain my denial any longer. Unbelievably, I really didn't feel a thing!! My fingers were numb and tingly: I could not even open a jar without a calamity. Could I be developing neuropathies? (More about that later.)

My Tai Chi class was held on Monday evenings. I had been taking and practicing Tai Chi since 2002 when my friend Yo and I first attended a class on a lark. What a great idea that turned out to be. Tai Chi helps with flexibility, strength, and memory, not to mention the boost it gives to your overall health. This oriental philosophy contends that Chi (Qi) is the body's life force. They believe that gathering and circulating good Chi, while eliminating bad Chi, promotes good health. Since I received my chemo every other Monday, I tried to make it to the class on my off week. My friend Leni not only encouraged me to go, but picked me up and brought me home when I couldn't drive.

I unquestionably reaped many benefits from Tai Chi, both physically and socially. Rick, our instructor and my personal healing guide, was wonderful during this time. He gave me modified movements to help stimulate the healthy Chi, as there were times when I could only sit on a chair and move just my extremities with the motions of the group. Keeping my breathing slow and easy, I followed as best as I could. When my body was accommodating, I would stand in the line-up and begin the segments of the form, moving with the group until it became necessary to sit down. At times my leg muscles would simply refuse to hold me up, and even my arms grew weary. Even so, I came away from these activities with a feeling of peace and empowerment. Tai Chi really helped me during my journey through Chemoland. I later learned that another woman in my Tai Chi group was going through chemotherapy, as well. Her lovely head scarves never gave her away. We chatted and soon formed a bond.

If there is an activity that you previously enjoyed—be it water aerobics, cards, a book group, or a club—stick with it. On the days you can, definitely give it a try, even if you only participate minimally. It can help you to get through this difficult time.

At each exam prior to chemo, Michele (Dr. Heim's Physician Assistant) would question me about any problems or side effects that I was experiencing. With the issues of diarrhea, wooziness, weakness, and blood pressure my litany remained constant. At each visit Michele would also ask if I had any signs of peripheral neuropathy. "Nope!" I would respond and vigorously shake my head, "I am doing just fine." These "neuropathies" result when toxic chemotherapy drugs damage sensitive nerve endings—usually in the hands and feet. The feet, in particular, can become so severely involved that they may feel like blocks of ice or wood. This overall loss of normal feeling is often accompanied by very painful sensations, as if rubber bands had been twisted tightly around the toes, ankles, and feet, depriving them of normal sensation. . The fingertips may also lose feeling, and this odd and painful sensation can gradually move up into the fingers and even parts of the hands. While many peripheral neuropathies resolve after chemotherapy is over, long-term damage can sometimes occur.

Every physician is concerned about patients developing neuropathies, and so will make an inquiry at each visit in order to identify the problem as quickly as possible. Be alert to any changes, no matter how subtle, as early awareness can be the key to reversing this condition down the road. At this stage of chemotherapy, Michele would also test me for peripheral neuropathy by laying pennies and dimes out on the desk and asking me to pick them up. For a while, I consistently picked them up without a problem. Later, I honestly thought I was fooling her when I turned my thumb on its side and pushed the edge of the given coin against my index finger, enabling me to lift it just enough for my numb fingers to grasp it. But I was only fooling myself!

One morning while I was downstairs, alone in the kitchen, I got a real inkling of just how devastating these neuropathies can be, and how their affect can strike you emotionally as well as physically. I reached for a coffee mug with my son, Zack's, college logo across it, a treasured gift from him and it somehow flew out of my grasp and shattered into a million pieces on the floor. That was my undoing. I literally had a meltdown and collapsed in tears on the floor. This brought Bob, my super-hero and hubby extraordinaire, on the run. After much back patting and comforting, which calmed me down, he assured me there would be a brand new one on the shelf the next morning—and there was. What a guy!

I seldom felt capable of driving myself anywhere, so I usually had someone with me when I went out. One day shortly before chemo number seven, I managed to take off on my own to the mall for some much needed retail therapy (as in shopping). All went well until a visit to a particular pit stop. I was in my favorite, and most often used, ladies room when I attempted to zip-up and leave the stall. I was shocked—I could not do it! I simply could not feel the zipper, so I couldn't grasp the teeny metal tab (something that I'd never previously given a second thought). How could something so familiar now evade me? It felt like trying to capture a hummingbird. The defiant metal seemed to retreat into the folds of my jeans, peeking out only to torment me. It was an unattainable task. After sweating over this new dilemma for several minutes, in a snit of frustration, I finally yanked out my tucked-in shirt and pulled it down over my gaping pants. It adequately covered me and I headed home with my tail between my legs and a pair of opened pants on my hips. It was time for revelations and, possibly, those elastic waist pants again.

Chapter 21

Revelations and Renovations

By this time, everything centered on my chemotherapy treatments and their aftermath. We had decided that after fifteen years in our home with very few changes, it was time for a cosmetic upgrade. So, we tore out the old indoor-outdoor carpeting in our laundry area and powder room, in order to replace it with ceramic tile. It was a great idea, since our two dogs had their food and water bowls there and clean up would now be much easier. Also, new tile would enhance the appearance. We planned on replacing our small out-dated vanity in the powder room with a larger modern one, as well. Because my most grueling side effects required quick access to the bathroom, that job had to be scheduled for late in my chemo cycle.

I somehow, (unbelievably) managed to tape off my stenciling, and with strength born of desire, painted the entire laundry area myself. The rich wheat color freshened up the room and would blend beautifully with the almond tiles I had chosen. I helped Bob install tile spacers, which leave room for the grout and even with meticulous planning, I still had to hurdle them in mini tiptoe fashion in order to meet my body's urgent demands for the bathroom. Can you imagine my anxiety when I learned that the fixtures would be removed and stored outside on the deck until the tile was down and set? The powder room was the only bathroom on the first floor. The next option would require a mad dash through the family room and kitchen, around the corner, down the hall, and up the stairs where, maybe, just maybe, I might make it to the guest bathroom.

With the expertise of a wedding planner, I now coordinated this small renovation, along with a much-anticipated visit from my Baltimore friends. Selecting the dates once again revolved around my chemotherapy. The tile was completed on September 17, but the powder and laundry rooms would not be accessible for at least four more days, to allow the tiles to properly set. Even so, I had plans for my friends to visit me on September 18 and 19—dates as far from chemo as possible. The next chemotherapy session, number seven, was scheduled for the following morning, September 20. Thankfully, the girls had no urgency problems (that I knew of) and should certainly be able to negotiate the stairs in a timely manner, whenever necessary.

I cleaned like a maniac: anticipation fueled me once again allowing me to override chemo's nagging reminders. Fortunately this visit included eating at some of our favorite places, so I did not have to chop, slice, or dice anything (including me). I was literally out in the middle of my street, waving madly like a five year old, when they finally pulled up. My face was split ear to ear by an irrepressible grin. After a warm homecoming of hugs and kisses we piled into the car and headed off to our favorite outdoor café. The weather was delightful and lunch was fabulous for them, and my soup at least hit the spot and seemed to stay with me. There was no way I could travel all the way to our usual spa in Hershey at the time, so we booked our treatments at a local, but very posh, spa just ten minutes from my house. In this way we upheld our yearly tradition, in spite of my situation.

I must be a slow learner. At the spa I relaxed with my feet encased in scented herbal wraps. Without thinking, I automatically reached for a tempting glass of wine. One sip of that putrid fuel reminded me soon enough! Do you think my pedicure girl noticed the pink tinge to the bubbling footbath? The girls grazed on fruits and cheeses while I nibbled a few grapes and kept my fingers crossed that I would not need to bolt to the ladies' room before my fuchsia tootsies were dry. Afterwards, we felt refreshed and pampered, all the way to the tips of our newly painted toes, and ready for more fun and indulgences. It meant so much to me to have my good friends drive all the way up here to share normal things with me during a not-so-normal time.

I willfully banned the weak and woozy twins while we shopped, and later that evening we had a truly memorable time. We ate at an original train station, converted into a beautiful, historic restaurant. It had been entirely restored, complete with marble floors and glass doors, which had at one time led to the tracks. The room was circled by mosaic tile murals depicting scenes of trains traveling through rolling landscapes. The ambiance was only outdone by the superb cuisine, and I even managed to enjoy half of my meal, saving the rest for later. We laughed and talked non-stop until weariness set in and finally sent us home. I knew I would miss them as they pulled away, but I would re-play the great memories for a long time to come, and dream of future get-a-ways.

After they left, our son's friend, Rick, came over and helped install the new pink and cream marble sink and . . . Hallelujah . . . the TOILET! He was my new hero, and the timing couldn't be better as the next morning we would be off for chemo number seven. I rejoiced in the knowledge that I could recuperate downstairs in my usual hide-a-way with a working bathroom nearby. Ah, the riches of life.

Getting ready that morning turned into a grueling task. My fingers and hands would not cooperate. Bob had to help me with my shoes and socks, as I just couldn't manage them. On the way out, I misjudged the single step from the kitchen to the family room, stumbled, and nearly crashed headfirst to the floor. Thankfully, Bob in his infinite wisdom and constant attention was holding onto me. I just didn't feel the edge of the step . . . something was not right! You think? Once we were at the center and had my port accessed and blood drawn, the next step in the journey was to see Michele for my pre-treatment exam. It went great, weight up, blood pressure down, and since I had been on Neulasta (to build up the white blood cell count) I felt confident that we would be off and running.

Next, out came the change . . . the pennies and dimes. *No problem*, I smugly thought, *time for the old side of the thumb trick*. Oh, but she must have had a trick of her own, because those coins were stuck fast to the desktop! Pick them up? I couldn't even feel them. The ever-present niggling worry about any possible cancer cell lingerers was suddenly overshadowed by the real probability of neuropathies. Once Michele revealed my true condition to Dr. Heim, he deleted the Oxaliplatin from this chemotherapy session. That is the drug that causes those strange reactions to cold temperatures . . . and is responsible for neuropathies. Just that one simple elimination, and my treatment was over much sooner than usual. We were out the door by 2:00 p.m.

I don't know if it was reality or just in my mind, but I actually felt much better with fewer side effects this time. During the next few weeks I became increasingly aware of the awful feeling—or lack of it—in my feet and toes. I had to be really vigilant now, when walking, as I could not distinguish drops in the pavement or feel the edges of steps. One afternoon, things really hit home. I squatted down to scoop dog food out of the big storage bin into Mookie and Bailey's bowls, as I did everyday. Thump! Halfway through, I landed smack on my ass! As if that wasn't bad enough, I also couldn't get back up, that sneaky chemo switched my strong legs for rubbery ones. I had to pull myself up, hand over hand, using the closet door for support. Incredible! I always thought I was such a strong woman, but not anymore—even if everyone kept telling me how strong I was now.

Chapter 22

Hanging On By Threads

As the number of chemotherapy treatments on board increased, the number of hairs on my head decreased. I knew, logically, that one of the side effects of chemotherapy might be hair loss, but I just didn't believe it would happen to me. While the chemo for bowel cancer does not cause complete baldness, it does decimate those rapidly multiplying hair follicles. The process causes a gradual detachment of the hair roots resulting in long hairs everywhere, on the pillow, on shirts, on the car seat, the couch—everywhere! I rationalized this latest discovery by telling myself, *It's only strands and not clumps.*

The results of this side effect were worse than both the dogs shedding in the summer. As much as I used to love brushing my long silky hair, that became an exercise in futility. It produced such anxiety that I whittled it down to a few mandatory strokes. I hated seeing my hairbrush grow fuzzy, laden with the displaced hairs, which were now repugnant to me. When I gently pulled my hair back and pinned it up, all appeared normal from the front, but my once lovely bun was reduced to the size of a jellybean. Thank goodness for kiddie barrettes.

As the months went, so did my hair. Prior to starting chemo, I bought a cute little pink baseball cap in a breathable material. It was to protect the skin on my face from the sun during chemo. The powerful chemo drug, 5-FU, intensifies the effects of the sun's burning rays, creating a less-than-desirable red and splotchy look. Now I broke out that cap again and wore it with the remaining strands of my hair framing my face. It looked like most of it was up under the cap, but actually very little of it was there.

Most of the time, I wore what I thought was my regular hair hanging down, mindless of the impact this made on others. One day on our way to book club, I asked my honest pal, Leni, if my hair looked okay down. She gave me a wry smile and simply said, "Put it up." This prompted me to make an appointment with my magical hairdresser, Joe. I reluctantly went to see him in the hopes he could conjure a head of hair for me. Oddly, I was a bit anxious about this appointment. I know, I must be nuts, after everything else, this worried me? First I told him no cutting, and then I meekly requested he treat my head like a baby's. Joe's gentle and talented hands made the most of a very limited situation. He was a better illusionist than David Copperfield. The rich golden colors made my hair appear a bit fuller and would look good (sure, hidden under a hat). He suggested cutting off those hanging strands of hair, but I was adamant about hanging onto those last few threads. I half-heartedly suggested, "I might consider it when I see some new growth."

A week after my eighth chemotherapy session, my best friend, Edie, in Baltimore was turning sixty. A surprise party was planned for her by her husband and family, and, of course, we were invited. Shopping for something to wear was fun and uplifting. The side effect of weight loss led to the purchase of smaller slacks, which would also serve me well during the remaining chemo sessions. While at the mall, I came across a black beret, and had a great idea! I combed my hair back with a swoop of bang showing, and jauntily tilted the beret on my head. No one would guess that those few delicate curls escaping from beneath the beret were all I had left! My brother, Norm, and his wife had sent me a gift of summer-weight and winter-weight berets, which I wore in Denver while my hair was just beginning to appear sparse. Now it seemed I could use a whole wardrobe of them.

This party meant so much to me, and Bob had been literally devoted to me during this period, so a compromise was in order. In northeast Pennsylvania, where we live, this was hunting season, so we agreed that Bob would hunt that morning, come home, clean his bird (assuming he got one!), and then shower and change in time to head south for the evening's activities. That night was my real beret debut, and the beginning of a fashion statement for me. Can you believe it? Someone who did not know me asked if I was a French model! I glibly responded, "Model, oh yeah, a model for chemotherapy!" Then I briefly reiterated my tale.

Despite being cloaked in toxins, and fearful of my body's shortcomings, I felt almost like my old self in the company of such good friends. I threw caution to the wind and sampled many of the tasty gourmet temptations. Some of my old favorites had come under the chemo sorcerers spell, turning them bitter, but so many others pleased my fickle palate that I really outdid myself. I lived in the moment, despite my husband's frequently raised eyebrows of concern. I had a great time, but paid the piper all night long! Oh well, such is chemo life.

It was a good thing we stayed at my friend, Sue's, in her beautifully decorated Laura Ashley loft with its private bathroom. Laura and I got rather intimate as I spent most of the night in that delicate floral sanctuary. It is amazing how much fluid the body can create. By morning, the meds had finally kicked in and I ate very tentatively from the smorgasbord that Sue laid out for her guests. Bob, with no gastronomic problems, ate well both the night before and that morning.

During our drive home we discussed the events of the previous evening and our wonderful time. He then brought up our up-coming thirtieth wedding anniversary. He said that by then (September 10) we would not only be celebrating thirty years of marriage, but my one-year cancer survivorship, as well. Those would be momentous occasions and Bob, once again, amazed me. He agreed to fulfill my life-long dream—we would go to Hawaii! Not only would we stay on Maui and take a cruise around the other Hawaiian Islands as well, but we planned to renew our vows at sunset on the beach in Maui. Just before chemo number ten I booked the trip, the dates were set, and this time we got travel insurance. It would be a dream come true!

The side effects were now accumulating like falling snow. I was having excessive diarrhea, often with water literally pouring out of me, and the weak and woozy twins came more often and stayed longer. Walking presented a problem with my feet feeling like two blocks of ice. I tripped easily and even fell down a few times. At my visit with Dr. Heim, it was time for full disclosure as my foot slipped getting up onto the scale . . . guess I didn't feel the edge? He decided that enough was enough. With ten treatments completed and only two remaining, I would have no more Oxaliplatin, and 15 percent less 5-FU (the big drug for the bowel that causes diarrhea) . . . HOORAY! While I fretted out loud about my neuropathies, Dr. Heim relieved some of my concerns, "Statistics have shown that people who become toxic have a better outcome, as they have not been under medicated during chemotherapy."

Shortly after chemo number eleven was completed and the pump was off, Bob left, with much coaxing from me, for his family hunting camp in the Allegheny National Forest. Before departing, he brought up, at my request, the enormous box filled with the gazillion parts needed to create our life-like Christmas tree. Then my friend, Yo, came over and the two of us spent literally the entire day assembling it, with much laughter and trial and error. After all, what would you expect from two Jewish girls, one with not-too-much feeling in her fingers? I tell you, "dahling," it looked "mahvelous" despite our belated discovery of a forgotten branch hidden in the bottom of the box (where it would stay hidden, until next year).

Bob returned in time for chemo number twelve, the last of this most intense round of chemotherapy. The morning of December 4 was perfect—crisp, clear, and very cool, but not quite cold yet. As we traveled to the chemo center for this last of the first big round, I contemplated the gorgeous crystalline sky, with not even a wisp of clouds to mar it, along with the wonderful man at the wheel, and life itself. I felt really excited, thrilled, and blessed that I was there. I believe that anyone who has walked in my shoes or traveled this journey with a loved one can relate to these emotions and would not deem me melodramatic—maybe not dramatic enough! Life itself has been quite the drama and I have treasured it, well, maybe not every moment . . .

Once again I toted gift bags, this time festooned with ribbons, Santas, and snowmen. Liz, Michele, and I shared tears and hugs, celebrating much more than the holidays. These remarkable women have had a profound and lasting affect on my life. My aggressive Dr. Heim will also never be forgotten, as his diligence and persuasion probably saved my life. My twelfth chemotherapy session went quickly with less 5-FU and no more Oxaliplatin, it actually seemed to give me a rush.

When we got home, I washed my recently tiled laundry and powder room floors, and, for good measure, I included the slate hall and foyer as well. All the while, my attached pump clicked and ticked, thumping my side in time with the strokes of the mop. Finally, everything was spotless and in readiness for the holidays. Unfortunately, the effort must have used up my entire energy supply for the next three days. I was spent, drained, and totally exhausted. I just needed to rest and recharge—whether from the effort or the chemo, it made no never-mind now.

December 13 marked a milestone—my six-month CT scan. I downed the prep with barely a second thought, and the procedure was a piece of cake. Afterwards, I was suddenly ravenous. I drove through Burger King and inhaled a whopper! (I'd never done that before!) The wait for the CT scan results, while ever-present in my thoughts, was pushed aside by wrapping, cooking, and general holiday prep. Zack would be coming home on December 19 . . . What a difference a year makes! Last December I was struggling with unknown demons, and this year I looked forward to the future. I thought that the gift of life (my CT results came back normal!) and love and family could not be beat, until the day after Christmas. .

That's when, we drove up to Karen and John's to celebrate and to visit with the whole family, Bob's dear Aunt Barb and Uncle Bud were there, too. The atmosphere was warm and loving and we were all having a wonderful time when an amazing thing happened. In perfect unison, Zack's cell phone and mine broke the reverie with their distinct tunes. What a surprise! Forcing her parents through a blizzard, my much-anticipated granddaughter, Rylie Elizabeth, who was not due until the beginning of January, arrived early and made the day complete. What a wonderful Christmas!

Chapter 23

The Last Blast

When we went to Sloan-Kettering Memorial Hospital for a second opinion, they recommended an additional six months of chemotherapy using only Avastin. This drug works in a unique way by destroying the circulation to cancer cells while causing fewer side effects than many of the other drugs. They cited statistics showing greatly reduced recurrence rates in patients following this protocol. (I learned much later that the dose would be tripled from that which I got during my first round of chemotherapy.)

The thought of six more months of the twins, weak and woozy, as well as many of their traveling companions, inhabiting my body was overwhelming. Continuing with chemotherapy for an entire year also meant carrying my Port-a-Cath in my chest . . . it's not as if it enhanced my profile or anything . . . When I dragged my feet about making this decision, my husband and both boys did more than give me a nudge in the right direction—they gave a shove! They did not encourage me so much as insist I continue with the six additional months of chemotherapy. No one wanted to give me a choice, insisting that they really needed their mom around and even the dogs, they contended, wanted their mommy to snuggle up to for a long time to come. Bob could hardly believe I might hesitate for an instant. They all, of course, did not have to get the drug, but it did feel good to hear such persuasive demands for my compliance.

Dr. Heim would be my last bastion in the decision-making process. I planned on asking him for a final opinion at my next check-up. After the lab work was reviewed at my check-up, and I was deemed healthy enough to proceed, I asked Dr. Heim what he would suggest if a member of his family were in the same boat. Obviously this was a no-brainer to everyone but the lucky recipient of six more months of chemo—me! So I signed on for the additional blast of chemo with the contingency that I would give my body time off for good behavior before starting the next round. My last chemo treatment of the first and most arduous session would be on December 4. With the holidays and Zack's upcoming visit in mind, we agreed that the first treatment of the next round would begin on January 2. What would I do with almost a whole month off?

Over the Christmas holiday I made a few discoveries, I bravely sampled a proffered alcoholic drink at my friend, Marie's. It was not rocket fuel at all, in fact, it was a rum and coke and quite tasty. This revelation led me to take another bold action. After months of mere "inhalation therapy," I submitted to the lure of a freshly perked cup of Christmas Blend coffee. AHHH, welcome home my old friend, caffeine! You were sorely missed.

This New Year's Eve was a real cause for celebration, because at that juncture I was deemed a six-month survivor. Despite snow and freezing temperatures, I dragged my old self out of the closet, aired her out, and dressed her up! I rang in the New Year in a suede mini-skirt, high-heeled boots, and a leopard top . . . Oh yeah, she's back! Shortly after midnight, the neighbors joined in my personal enthusiasm and swept me up in a celebratory march around the room. I was held aloft by all the handsome hubbies except for mine, who quite considerately made it through the midnight kissing and toasting before he slid away—ostensibly to let the dogs out, but in reality, to get some sleep.

Cautious imbibing, great friends, and my wonderful husband and sons, carried me into 2007! On the morning of January 2, true to my form, I stopped and got my nails done; something I was unable to do during all of chemotherapy, beyond the first few treatments. My fingernails, much like everything else, were affected by the drugs. They split length-wise and developed nasty brown discolorations covering the whole nail—not too attractive. So, I stopped getting manicures for the six months of chemo.

Now things were beginning to improve and it was very liberating to resume even this small normal activity.

My friend, Kathy B's shop was right on the way, so, I literally killed two birds with one stone. First I got fresh pink nails with sparkly snowflakes and then I got the potent golden drug, Avastin. What a delightful surprise! Chemo was over in an hour! For this round, treatments would be scheduled once every three weeks. *Boy,* I thought to myself smugly, *I can do that standing on my head!* At home that first day after my Avastin, I was freezing cold and nauseated (nothing new there). The weirdest sensation came over me when trying to talk or walk. I felt like I was under water, making everything much more difficult. Medication, blankets, and rest did the trick, and three days later I went out with Leni and Yo to breakfast and a movie. Breakfast and a movie, three days after my chemotherapy! Wow, unbelievable!

On March 8, just two days after my fourth Avastin treatment, Bob and I left together for Denver to visit Jeremy and to meet our granddaughter. How different this visit was! Oh, I still had lots of problems, like tons of diarrhea (which I handled with Imodium), exhausting fatigue, and neuropathy that gripped my hands and feet in its icy clenches. So, I walked cautiously and didn't handle knives. Holding a baby in your arms, especially your new granddaughter is the best medicine imaginable. Despite my many issues, this trip was wonderful. I even managed to cook and enjoy a big family dinner, as my brother, Norm, flew out to see his new little great-niece and his "old big sis."

About two weeks after that trip, on March 26, my Baltimore girls came up again for our annual visit. This time, however, we were able to shop 'til we dropped, and hang out at our local haunts. Food and drinks were back on my menu. After breakfast at our favorite diner, the Gourmet, we headed down to the Hershey Spa for our personal indulgences. My old standby complaints became routine until our trip. Then I developed something new—a sharp immobilizing pain in my shoulder that emerged while performing the non-strenuous act of reaching behind me to pull out a sheet of toilet paper. OUCH! That really hurt! Other than that, I felt pretty good, and even jogged a bit on the treadmill in the gym. (I just couldn't swing my arm much.) I ate cautiously, but at last I really ate! I had my favorite dish—rack of lamb with caramelized onions and garlic potatoes, washed down with a fine Merlot. This was a great trip for many reasons but mostly it was a partial reclamation of me.

During chemotherapy I pondered my return to nursing. Toward the end of my treatments, the idea really took hold. While nursing part-time at the hospital, long before my involuntary time-out for chemo, I had also picked up a few days at a freestanding surgery center, but, coincidently, they closed down at about the time I was diagnosed. When I heard that my old surgery center planned on reopening, I had Bob personally deliver my resume while I received my next Avastin treatment.

I was given another gift when I met with John, the new director for an interview. There I was, somewhat professionally dressed, but with a beret on my head. I explained my situation and added that by the time of the proposed re-opening I would be finished with my chemotherapy. How fortuitous for me that John's wife had also gone through chemotherapy, and was now doing well (though still plagued by neuropathies). He hired me as a post-operative (recovery room) nurse, starting out at one day a week until I was back to normal and their needs increased. The neuropathies in my feet actually seemed to be improving ever so slightly, and the area involved on my left foot had receded to encompass only the toes and about one-forth of the lower foot. My troublesome right foot was down to being about half involved, which was an improvement of sorts, though the sensation still ranged from tight and constricted to a painful frozen feeling. I had to exercise caution when walking, going up or down stairs, and most importantly, when purchasing shoes. On one of my shopping forays, I came upon a pair of white nursing shoes with Velcro closures. What a break for me, as they were comfortable—though not much of a fashion statement for someone over the age of five. Thus armed, I began my orientation at the new surgery center on April 9, Port-a-Cath in place, with only a month and a half of chemo remaining! It would surely be smooth sailing from this point on. Right?

On April 19, after my chemo treatment was finished I experienced chest pains. This brought me back, full cycle, to my cardiologist's office, where it all began. Apparently Avastin not only caused a spike in blood pressure, but it produced chest pains, too. I learned from Dr. Ross that he also had to go to the hospital for chest pains while receiving his chemotherapy. Vigilance by my steadfast cardiologist and blood pressure medication helped control this latest problem. Even though I was still haunted by many side effects, especially those involving the G.I. tract, I felt my self slowly growing stronger.

At the end of April, my brave friend Karen (of the "snake creeps up" adventure) and I took a long awaited trip to Washington D.C. While exploring the nation's capitol we decided to take the subway. Once inside the station, chemo's demands forced their way into our plans . . . urgently! Luckily for me there was a very kind police attendant on duty who sympathized with my plight and unlocked their personal restroom just in a nick of time. This was fun but a very active trip, requiring lots of walking. It really tested my mettle and I rose to the occasion every day. Only once, when our daily cumulative mileage was well over the ten-mile mark, did I cave in. I opted to sit out the hike up the unending stairs to the Lincoln Monument. I might have been too pooped to pop, but I had seen it already, anyway, and the marble bench beckoned.

Without any lifting or rigorous movement, my shoulder pain was bearable, but the slightest use would set off an immobilizing pain that took forever to calm down. I wondered just what the chemo may have done. I reluctantly made an appointment to see my orthopedic doctor when I got home. I just hated the thought of one more doctor's appointment, but I knew it was now a necessity. There were several things for me to look forward to upon our return. My one year CT scan was scheduled, along with my birthday, the anniversary of my one year survivorship, and my last chemo treatment—all fell in the month of May. I couldn't wait for spring! It would hold one ending and many new beginnings.

Chapter 24

A Magical Milestone Morning

May 1 marked my one year CT scan. Aside from the emotional repercussions of waiting for the results, it was not much worse than going to the dentist. The next day I was headed south to Baltimore, not only to be with my dear friends but also to celebrate my *fortieth* reunion from nursing school! It did not seem possible that I had been a nurse for forty years . . . much less be that old! I forged ahead with the exciting events, tucking my pathetic strands under a beret and planting a smile on my lips. Hey I was there, eager, and alive! The days spun away in a whirlwind of laughter, food, and drink, and of course, remembering. The trip was wonderful, but the icing on the cake was the news I received upon my return home. My CT scan was normal! I felt lighter, and even the air around me seemed brighter. A giant sigh escaped from me, and the world was again a great place. CT scans and blood work are the cancer survivors' hallmarks of health.

On the morning of May 10, Bob and I left bright and early and traveled west across Pennsylvania to the Allegheny National Forest. Our destination was Bob's family cabin, hidden in the woods there. We met his cousin, Jim, and his wife, JoAnn (also a cancer survivor), to share this important weekend. We warmed ourselves by the crackling bonfire, enjoyed perfect company, and perfect steaks at our campsite banquet, complete with a delicious dessert of S'mores.

The next day would be most special for me . . . May 11, 2007 . . . one full year. The following are the words I wrote in my notebook that day:

May 11, 2007

I slipped from my cozy nest of blankets into the early spring chill and filled my lungs with pure, unpolluted forest air. A melodic symphony played by songbirds filtered through the open windows, as the tinkle of wind chimes mimicked the percussion section of nature's orchestra. I peered out the window and was treated to a sky tinted with the delicate strokes of sunrise. The lingering edge of deep navy was delicately trimmed in peach and apricot, while mandarin and bright gold slashed across the horizon, heralding a beautiful day ahead.

Rich aromatic scents of freshly brewed coffee danced in the air and tantalized my newly awakened taste buds. The guys stealthily left the cabin in the wee hours, concealed by the forest's cloak of darkness, to hunt turkeys. I mentally thanked them for the steaming pot of coffee left in their wake.

Shafts of sunlight pierced the dense darkness as their glowing fingers of gold separated the night from day. Mother Nature's call and the welcoming light of dawn nudged me out of the cabin. During my quick jaunt to the outhouse, I became aware of my heightened senses, as the soft velvety coats on the rocks tickled my bare feet. Interspersed among them were wild Trilliums with their rosy faces tilted up towards the sun, creating a natural floral brocade. When the rays of morning light struck minerals embedded in the rock surfaces, the forest floor was illuminated by nature's twinkling LCDs. The gurgling spring rushed to meet the brook as they babbled away in their own language.

On my way back to the cabin, my reverie was broken by hummingbirds diving in front of my face as they raced to a nectar-laden feeder. I padded into the quiet kitchen area and poured a mug of the dark brew, inhaling the seductive scent before that first welcome sip. My hands held the mug and my ever-present notebook, where I had been recording the events and emotions of the past year—my memoirs.

As I sat at the round antique table with its claw-ball feet, I was mesmerized by the beauty of the woods just beyond the picture window. The hummingbirds flitted back and forth to the feeder, as rays of light reflected off their tiny bodies, fragmenting into ruby, emerald, and pearl gems.

My thoughts meandered over the past year, stopping at today's momentous milestone. The date was Friday, May 11, 2007 and I was a one-year cancer survivor. Is it possible I was different, changed like a chrysalis that evolves into a butterfly? Was I altered forever, mentally and physically? Perhaps, but I was still me, with so many hopes, dreams, and adventures to pursue. I felt good, gaining strength and endurance, and have walked miles with no stomach pains or shortness of breath. My healed incision, a remarkable faint four-inch line etched into my belly, is still evident between my right hipbone and my navel. It reminds me of all that I have to be grateful for. (Thank you, Dr. DelSerra, for your small hands and wonderful tailoring.) Neuropathies still plague my fingertips and feet. Yet, optimistically, I think that this too shall pass.

Today I am cancer free, and am getting on with life. I have one final chemotherapy treatment to complete this journey of almost one year. After receiving ten drugs every other week, reduced to just one drug every three weeks, I really can't say, "I endured this." Perhaps it would be more fitting to say I accepted it, or tolerated it, or maybe, I just got it done! I am a new grandma and an old nurse, married to the same, yet dramatically changed man, for almost thirty years. Thinking about him I am surprised by a burst of old feelings and strong emotional charges. They race through me without warning or provocation, stimulating nerve endings head to toe, stopping right in the middle . . . it is profound love!

The trip to Denver was wonderful, this time with Bob as a new grandpa. I have held and cuddled my new granddaughter, and have hugged and laughed with both my sons. Thanks so much for this, my children. This year closed the distance, drawing my two brothers into my life. They live on two separate coasts, yet I have been with both of them, hugged them, and talk to them weekly. Stu and Norm, you have been there for me through this most difficult and challenging year. Thank you both for your concern and support, medical advice, elastic pants, and stylish berets.

Zack, my baby (I'm sorry, even though you are an adult, you always will be to me), I hope you know what your constant connection to me has meant. Your often twice daily calls served not only as a sounding board, but were like a beacon of light cutting through the darkness. Your research, knowledge and suggestions were monumental, thank you for being who you are. Jeremy, my first born, we weathered some rough times and trials and errors. I was so young but did the best I knew how. I have always loved you and always will, and no one can take your place. I feel blessed to have the chance to be in your life. Thank you for your visits and for sharing your home and yourself with me, and for catering to me during my tough time. Boys, I could not have written this book without the patient tutelage and unlimited technical support you both gave!

Last weekend I was fortunate to be able to attend my nursing school reunion. The years fell away as we entered a time warp and relived our twenty-something nursing school adventures. I expected to be with a bunch of sixty-year-old females, not these beautiful, strong, intelligent women. I give thanks for that opportunity, and for all of my wonderful friends.

My mind returns to the verdant forest as a rush of peace and tranquility flows over me. I give thanks for blue skies, fresh air, beautiful get-a-ways with my wonderful husband, and the chance to enjoy it all—and, most importantly, for my life. I finished my coffee as the sun stripped the forest of her dark veil, and I rushed out to the picnic table in an attempt to record these thoughts while they were still fresh. I plan on including this in my memoir, just as I write it today.

I hope what I have shared with you has moved you, made you laugh, and most of all, helped you to cope. I know that writing this has been cathartic and therapeutic for me. My sincere hope is that it may help you, or someone you care about, in some small way. Tomorrow is my sixty-first birthday: last year I was on my back in shock and agony, the ramifications of the year ahead unknown to me. Today, surrounded by the natural beauty of the forest, I dream . . . No, not dream, but plan and organize a wish-come-true—our trip to Hawaii. We will go in September, to celebrate our thirtieth anniversary and my survival.

Today, I celebrate life and one year clear, and tomorrow, my birthday; will be just that, the birth and beginning of the rest of my life.

Chapter 25

Fairy Tales Can Come True

My recent milestone was celebrated in magical surroundings, convened with nature, and deeply introspective. That weekend left me walking on air, feeling alert and happy, even though my shoulder was still really hurting me. I was eager to complete my chemotherapy and get on with my life. My desire to be as normal as possible was reinforced, which meant a visit to the orthopedic physician. I reluctantly got the MRI he ordered prior to the appointment; just one more medical necessity. My shoulder pain was finally diagnosed. As I had suspected, it revealed a partial tear of a ligament. I was certain that chemotherapy was the culprit, but if so, I'll say once again, it was a small price to pay.

A steroid injection into the joint sent me home with dramatically less pain. I followed the physical therapy protocol given to me and gradually regained the usage of my arm. With each passing day my spirits soared as the mobility in my arm increased. With my shoulder vastly improved, I returned to work in the recovery area at the surgery center, and I also did some school nursing. Bob and I purchased our summer flowers and I filled flower boxes on the deck and planted the barrels in our front yard.

The profusion of colors heralded the arrival of spring—it was coming, and so was Zack, life was good. Everything seemed to cooperate with us, the weather was great, and we had a wonderful visit. Zack got to go fishing and visit friends, as well as spend quality time at home. On May 29 he accompanied us to my last chemotherapy treatment. After it was completed, we went to the most beautiful restaurant in the area and had a scrumptious lunch. Even I enjoyed it, for a change. Luckily, we saved enough room for ice cream sundaes at the local dairy farm where their ice cream was produced. The sun was warm, the sundaes were sweet, and the time, as always flew by swiftly.

Finally that bittersweet moment arrived, as we took Zachary to the airport the next day. I was finished with chemotherapy and ready to follow my dream. Our trip to Hawaii was booked, and we were leaving on Labor Day, Monday, September 3. Despite fatigue, neuropathies, and GI disturbances, I resumed my normal activities and more. My blood pressure slowly leveled off and, per my doctor's suggestion, I stopped taking the medication for that. Bob and I were walking literally miles, we even worked up to a five-mile route.

I guess we were both eating healthier and getting lots of exercise that summer because Bob took his job as caregiver very seriously. He kept me in fruits and vegetables, as well as encouraging walking. These are great activities for everyone, especially cancer survivors. As my body worked hard to restore normalcy, my hair gave up completely. A few strands still hung down here and there, but just enough to keep me in denial until two weeks before our trip. How strange, after everything I had been through, that I was feeling anxious on my way downtown to meet with Joe, my hairdresser extraordinaire.

Patti met me there (I had introduced her to him earlier) for moral support and to man the camera. I have had long hair since the ninth grade when my mom cut my hair in what was then called a "pixie" many decades ago. Other than trimming or shaping, I have never really cut my hair since then, actually wearing it to my waist (a la Cher) until I was almost forty. Once in the chair, with my hair shampooed and rinsed, I realized it was just a matter of a few snips and I had a short cap of softly curled hair. ("Chemo curls"; I'd always had pin-straight hair.) Joe worked his magic and, while it was short—really short—it looked better and healthier, though quite different. A pedicure and a manicure with tiny orchids completed my beauty preparations for the trip.

I pondered the idea of having my Port-a-Cath surgically removed before our departure. Dr. Heim suggested at least a six-month waiting period after the last chemo treatment, so I dismissed that idea for the time being. At least it was completely waterproof and safely nestled beneath my skin, so I could still do anything I was physically capable of without worrying about it.

I was different, though changed in more ways than short hair and neuropathies. I was a cancer survivor with one year under my belt and a marriage of almost thirty years: both cause for celebration.

On Monday, September 3, we departed for Maui, and after a day of travel we arrived safely in paradise. It was 9:00 p.m. in Maui and 4:00 a.m. for us, so we didn't see much on our ride from the airport to the hotel. The air itself was warm and balmy, heavy with the sweet scent of tropical flowers. Each day revealed another exciting aspect of this beautiful island. The first evening we went to a Hawaiian luau with authentic Hawaiian music, dance, food, and drink. We partook of the traditional pig roasted in a pit in the sand (Emu) and covered with wet palm leaves, after which we toasted each other with frothy Mai Tais. The dancing hula girls had Bob's undivided attention while I was raptly entertained by the glistening men with their big fiery swords. OH YEAH! We toured the historic port town of Lahina and ate dinner overlooking the Pacific Ocean in the famous restaurant, Cheeseburger in Paradise.

Thursday at two in the morning, we layered ourselves with warm outerwear as we prepared for our pre-dawn adventure. A van picked us up at the hotel and transported us to the top of Haleakala Volcano to watch the earth's most glorious sunrise. The elevation was so high there that the early morning temperature was freezing. Among vivid cloud formations, the first blazing tongues of the sun appeared as if fire in a dragon's mouth. It was totally breath taking! Once the sun was up, we put on our helmets and gloves and hopped on the mountain bikes brought up with the van. Our guide checked us out for a thirty-six mile downhill adventure to the bottom of the volcano and a local eatery where we had a Hawaiian breakfast.

The *pièce de résistance* came at sunset on Friday evening, our last night on Maui. According to our plans, we met a local minister at the base of Black Rock, a volcanic formation rising thirty feet above a most beautiful stretch of powdery beach. I wore a white eyelet sundress, bare feet, and a flower in my hair. Bob had on a softly hued Hawaiian shirt and khaki shorts. Right at sunset, with Black Rock and the final glory of the sun dropping into the ocean as a backdrop, we faced each other and renewed our vows in honor of our thirtieth anniversary. The minister conducted a moving ceremony that included an exchange of leis and the Hawaiian version of the Unity Candle. We each were instructed to scoop up a handful of sand together and, as he intoned the blessings, we simultaneously poured them into a special flask. Our emotional recitation of the vows we had secretly written to each other brought us both to tears.

This memorable occasion was concluded with a kiss, an embrace, and the pop of a bottle of champagne that we brought to the beach. Friends we had met at the pool earlier in the week were our witnesses, as well as our photographers. I had known the parents of one of these friends from Baltimore for many years. In fact, I had helped his mother deliver his brother many years ago when I first worked in the delivery room. What a small world! They were in Hawaii on their honeymoon!

As we sipped our champagne, crisp and bubbly, I got another surprise. Earlier that day, while lounging at the pool, a man carried his daughter out of the ocean with her foot dripping blood. My pediatric nurse instincts kicked in, and in the absence of a doctor I ran over and immediately assessed the situation. She had sustained a long deep slice in the bottom of her foot, either from sharp coral, or from the fin of a too-friendly fish. I held pressure on her laceration, got ice, towels, and the hotel's first-aid kit. After several minutes of pressure, I suggested to the dad that he take her to the nearby infirmary where they could see if she required stitches. I applied a pressure dressing that temporarily stopped the bleeding, and off they went in the hotel-provided golf cart.

As we left the beach that evening, I noticed the little girl at the top of the steps. She was in a wheelchair with her foot elevated and freshly bandaged, with her dad beaming next to her. She needed seven stitches, and the doctor told them I had done a fine job of stopping the bleeding and holding the wound closed. They shared in our joy and she gave me a hug and a beautiful memento from Maui, which I will always treasure.

The next morning we flew to Honolulu where we boarded a cruise ship to begin a weeklong cruise to the major Hawaiian Islands. Each day was filled with more excitement and adventure including: kayaking the inland waters of Kauai, driving the impossible road to Hanna, walking along the rim of a still-active volcano, and climbing down a mountain path to swim under a golden waterfall. I even managed to fit hula lessons into our demanding schedule. While cruising at sea on September 10, the exact date of our anniversary, we had a fantastic dinner that ended with serenading waiters and a miniature cake just for us, complete with our names and best wishes. At last we pulled into port with the arrival of the morning sun, and finished the champagne and the last of our cake. Pearl Harbor lay in the distance, as our next and final destination on this incredible journey. Tanned and radiant, our arms wrapped around one another, we kissed one more time and relished the trip that had proved that fairy tales can come true.

Epilogue

I worked on this book while chemo worked on me, I worked on this book while my body worked on itself, and I worked on it when I was, once again, myself. I am changed, of course. Anyone who has been diagnosed with cancer will be changed. But those changes, be they physical (and there will be plenty of those) or emotional, cannot alter who you are. You may feel that you have become a better, more aware and caring person than before cancer. Deep bonds of friendship and support may be formed, and family ties strengthened. Some people may have found a new spirituality, or may have pursued dreams that had been held in abeyance for various reasons. I personally fit into all of these categories.

My journal served as a catalyst to recreate the thoughts and feelings I experienced during the year-long search and the following year of chemotherapy. Many people have referred to me as brave, strong, or even stoic, yet I never thought of myself in any of those terms. When I look back, it amazes me how tough my travels through Chemoland were at times. It just never seemed that way to me. Perhaps, I simply never analyzed what I was going through, but only focused on getting it done?

In the month following my first year anniversary as a survivor, Bob and I attended a Survivor's Celebration. It was a wonderful event bringing cancer survivors and their caregivers together with others, in a joyous celebration of life. Following this, I became a member of the committee to develop the next year's event. Bob eventually joined me and we both volunteered at the celebration held right after my second anniversary as a survivor. (The date of your diagnosis will become a major milestone in your life.) We will continue to lend our time and support to the Northeast Regional Cancer

Institute for as long as they can use us. NRCI (Northeast Regional Cancer Institute) recently published my survivor story in their newsletter. Reading that article triggered my desire to complete this memoir.

During my year-and-a-half exam and visit with Dr. Heim, we discussed the possibility of having my Port-a-Cath removed. As this was now more than the six months he had suggested, he saw no reason not to move forward and schedule that procedure. I know many people that have actually kept their Port-a-Caths intact and functioning for many months, even years, after completing chemotherapy. When I discussed this with them I got the feeling it seemed to be their "Talisman" and its presence could ward off evil. (Cancer?) Yet, I wanted mine removed, felt that it had served me well, and would simply no longer be needed.

On December 5, 2007, I awoke at 6:30 a.m. with a thrill of excitement, which was at times overshadowed by a thread of anxiety. On my way to the shower, as I passed by the mirror and glanced over—was it my imagination—or did my port wink a secret little goodbye to me? At 8:00 a.m. that morning, I was so quickly whisked into the OR, with absolutely no problems (not with permits, or IVs, or anything!) that I had a little difficulty believing it was true. By 1:00 p.m. I was relaxing back at home on that famous couch, not in a cocoon state but excited and relieved to have my Port-a-Cath removed. (Yes, of course, I still have it . . . but in a specimen jar, not *in me!*) It served me faithfully, with never a moment of failure, but having it removed was a major step to closure. I really felt very little discomfort and kept touching that little spot for reassurance that I did not just imagine it being gone. (I still do from time to time)

I had my two-and-a-half-year CT scan and blood work done, and the results were all normal. A survivor will be on a health maintenance schedule set up by their oncologist. It is similar to the routine appointments for your vehicle to keep it in tip-top running order. I still have neuropathies in my feet, the right much worse than the left, but my fingertips are greatly improved (I even handle knives again). Perhaps this too, will pass, or not . . .

I have been working at least one day a week at the surgery center, and I get to the pediatric unit at the hospital occasionally, as well as a few days here and there doing school nursing. So, I guess one would say that I am functioning normally. I continue with Tai Chi and my reading group (maybe someday they can discuss this book?), while managing a very busy social calendar as well. Bob retired after thirty-four years in law enforcement, and we spent the summer months walking regularly. We even logged seventy miles during the month of August.

My current weight, despite a year of chemotherapy, is pretty good, but now I have to watch my intake in order to keep those unwanted pounds in check. Eating healthily has become second nature to both of us. Any cancer survivor should include lots of fruits and vegetables in their diet, as well as some exercise in their daily regimen. My gifted hairdresser, Joe, can really work magic now that he has a little more to work with! I wear my hair just below my jaw in a swingy, current style. I hope to be able to wear it up again for work in the future, when I will finally see my complete old self reflected in the mirror (sans Port-a-Cath).

Early this December I participated in a local playhouse rendition of "It's a Wonderful Life." (It is!) Fortunately, the format was that of a forties' radio show, so I did not have to memorize (I'm not sure that I could have), but read from the script instead. It was fun and stimulated my sluggish brain cells. Just before Christmas my son, Jeremy, flew east and met his brother in Baltimore. Then they drove up to Pennsylvania for a visit with us. This was the first Christmas (and Chanukah) in many years that we had both boys at home and it was very special. Grandma, (she calls me "MiMi"), grandpa, and uncle Zack even got to spend time with Rylie, celebrating the holidays and her second birthday. It is amazing what can transpire in a couple of years.

It is my hope to become a patient advocate and help others in a similar situation. If you managed a smile while reading, or if anything you have read in this memoir helped you, or someone you know, then I have realized my dream.

* * *

Franie's Checklist and Trip-Ticket

Before Chemotherapy/Surgery:

- ☐ Discuss pain management options (pump, pills, etc) with your physician.
- ☐ Get copies of your CT scans, x-rays, blood tests, and pathology reports.
- ☐ Make a list of all your current medications (prescriptions, vitamins, herbal supplements, and sleeping pills).
- ☐ Obtain a small camping-style pillow (to hold against your incision when you move).
- ☐ Get a second opinion at a cancer center.

During Chemotherapy:

- ☐ Ask your doctor about using EMLA Cream.
- ☐ Dress comfortably; consider elastic waist or drawstring pants, and a tank or tube top to help with port access.
- ☐ Take a warm sweatshirt or sweater and socks.
- ☐ Bring along a neck pillow.

Things to Include in a Tote Bag:

- ☐ Hand lotion, lip balm, lollipops, and tissues;
- ☐ A journal, pen, letters, books, and magazines;
- ☐ Knitting, crossword puzzles, and your favorite hand-held video games.

Pack a Cooler:

- ☐ Gatorade, bottled water, twist-cap soda, or juice;
- ☐ Dry snacks, cookies, crackers, chips, raisins;
- ☐ Single-serve Jell-o cups, pudding cups, fruit cups;
- ☐ Sandwiches (try peanut butter for a sweet tooth, and cheese to cover any salt cravings).

Breinigsville, PA USA
02 March 2010
233400BV00003B/2/P